The Leader's Guide to Managing People

The Leader's Guide to Managing People

How to use soft skills to get
hard results

Mike Brent and Fiona Elsa Dent

Harlow, England • London • New York • Boston • San Francisco • Toronto • Sydney • Auckland • Singapore • Hong Kong
Tokyo • Seoul • Taipei • New Delhi • Cape Town • São Paulo • Mexico City • Madrid • Amsterdam • Munich • Paris • Milan

PEARSON EDUCATION LIMITED

Edinburgh Gate
Harlow CM20 2JE
United Kingdom
Tel: +44 (0)1279 623623
Web: www.pearson.com/uk

First published 2014 (print and electronic)
© Mike Brent and Fiona Elsa Dent 2014 (print and electronic)

The rights of Mike Brent and Fiona Elsa Dent to be identified as authors of this work have been asserted by them in accordance with the Copyright, Designs and Patents Act 1988.

Pearson Education is not responsible for the content of third-party internet sites.

ISBN: 978-0-273-77945-2 (print)
       978-0-273-78037-3 (PDF)
       978-0-273-78036-6 (ePub)
       978-1-292-00744-1 (eText)

British Library Cataloguing-in-Publication Data
A catalogue record for the print edition is available from the British Library

Library of Congress Cataloging-in-Publication Data
Brent, Mike.
  The leader's guide to managing people : how to use soft skills to get hard results / Mike Brent and Fiona Elsa Dent.
    pages cm
  Includes bibliographical references and index.
  ISBN 978-0-273-77945-2 (pbk. : alk. paper)
  1. Leadership. 2. Personnel management. 3. Communication in management. 4. Interpersonal relations. 5. Teams in the workplace--Management. I. Dent, Fiona Elsa. II. Title.
  HD57.7.B74824 2014
  658.3--dc23
                          2013036642

10 9 8 7 6 5 4 3 2
17 16 15 14

Print edition typeset in 9pt Melior by 3
Print edition printed and bound in Great Britain by Ashford Colour Press Ltd., Gosport, Hampshire

NOTE THAT ANY PAGE CROSS REFERENCES REFER TO THE PRINT EDITION

Dedicated to our parents,
Stephen and Angela Brent,
Ena and Gordon Campbell

Contents

Contents

About the authors

Mike Brent is a Client and Programme Director at Ashridge Business School. He specialises in leadership, team building, influencing, coaching, cross-cultural management, leading change and personal development. His interests include how to foster self-awareness and creativity, and how to challenge effectively.

Mike has worked as a management trainer and consultant with many international companies, such as GE, HP, Ericsson, France Telecom, ICI, Volvo and Bang and Olufsen, and has a particular interest in working with management teams. He has extensive international experience, having run seminars worldwide, including in Japan, China, Uzbekistan, Thailand, Malaysia, Indonesia, the US, Canada and South America.

Mike has published a number of articles and two books on influencing, coaching and leadership, including the book, *Influencing – Skills and Techniques for Business Success*, with Fiona Dent.

Fiona Dent is an independent trainer, coach and Associate Faculty at Ashridge. Her previous experience was as Director of Executive Education at Ashridge where she was involved in setting the strategic direction of the organisation with a particular focus on human resources. She also managed programmes, client relationships and delivered management development solutions in the leading people area.

Fiona has worked with a range of organisations and clients on a national and international basis, and teaches and consults across a broad spectrum of leadership, personal, interpersonal and relationship skills.

Fiona has written seven books and she continues to write and research in the areas of influence, relationship management and women in business. For more information about Fiona, see her website: **www.feddevelopment.co.uk**.

Mike and Fiona are authors of the bestselling FT Publishing title, *The Leader's Guide to Influence.*

Acknowledgements

In particular we would like to express our appreciation to those people who actively contributed to our reflections, especially the many managers and leaders we work with, and who shared their experiences with us.

Thanks also to the following people: Nigel Melville, Greg Searle, Andrew Ktoris, Evan George and his colleagues at Brief, Mark McKergow, Jenny Clarke, Paul Z. Jackson, Professor Shelly Gable, Masesi Malongete, Jean Pierre Loiseau, Guy Mansfield, Davide Dardanello, Charlotte Sills, Kate McCourt and Sarah Qing Tian.

Additionally we would like to thank our Ashridge colleagues for their help and support, especially Viki Holton, Sharon West, Alex Davda, Kerrie Fleming and Phil Anderson for their practical support.

Finally, we would like to thank our editor at Pearson, Nicole Eggleton.

Publisher's acknowledgements

We are grateful to the following for permission to reproduce copyright material:

Figures

Figure 4.2 adapted from GRRROW model, with permission from Sir John Whitmore; Figure 7.1 adapted from 'Second thoughts on team building', *Management Education and*

Development, Vol. 15, pp. 163–175 (Critchley, B. and Casey D. 1984); Figures 7.2 and 7.3 from Tuckman, Bruce W., 'Developmental sequence in small groups', *Psychological Bulletin*, 63, pp. 384–399, American Psychological Association, adapted with permission; Figure 7.4 The Margerison-McCann Team Management Wheel is a registered trademark. Reproduced by kind permission of TMS Development International Ltd, 2013 **www.tmsdi.com**; Figure 14.1, Professor Shelly Gable, University of California.

In some instances we have been unable to trace the owners of copyright material, and we would appreciate any information that would enable us to do so.

Introduction

Before you are a leader, success is all about growing yourself. When you become a leader, success is all about growing others.

Jack Welch

L eading people is a social skill. We believe that the key to effective people leadership in organisations is to move the focus away from the logical, impersonal and unemotional approaches that many organisations encourage and managers practise, and get back to the basic human dimensions of relationship and cooperation.

We see leaders as enablers of people, as skilled at reading and understanding others, able to tune into their people's inner thoughts and motivations, and to use these skills both to enable effective performance in the workplace and to increase the satisfaction and pleasure that employees find in their job. Social anthropologist Michael Tomasello says we are all social and emotional creatures. As such we need to be able to leverage these social and emotional aspects to ensure both job satisfaction and performance.

In the past, the focus of management has been on the individual, but we forget that companies are above all relational entities. We therefore feel it is essential for managers to improve their relational and psychological skills in order to become the most effective managers and leaders they can be.

This book is clearly advocating that to lead people effectively, managers must become like psychologists and be able to go beyond the obvious and external and delve into the internal motivations and thoughts of their people. We will not focus on quantitative tools and techniques, but on aspects such as the emotional self-control of the manager, their ability to tune into and understand their people's thoughts and motivations, their ability to empathise, understand and, crucially, help their people learn and develop so they can achieve their full potential.

Does this sound too wishy-washy? Too unrealistic? Let's look, then, at what's happening at the UK's biggest supermarket chain, Tesco. This retailer, although still generating healthy profits worldwide, has been seen to have 'dropped the ball' in its UK operation. Chief executive officer (CEO) Philip Clarke has been making some interesting statements recently and has gone on record saying he will put the heart and soul back into Tesco. Heart and soul: since when did one of the FTSE 100 bosses start talking about heart and soul? So how will he put the heart and soul back into Tesco? In a recent article in the *Sunday Times* he said: 'Workers will be encouraged to be more friendly.'

> To lead people effectively, managers must become like psychologists

It seems that Mr Clarke has understood that we are indeed a relational species and that Tesco customers want empathy and friendliness as well as low prices.

The late Peter Drucker, one of the world's leading thinkers and writers on management, said that management is about human beings and that its task is to make people capable of joint performance and to make their strengths effective and their weaknesses irrelevant.

So the journey in this book will be a relational and emotional one. We will look at how we can improve your people skills at work and how improving them will make you a much more effective leader of people.

The people leadership model

Leading and managing people is a complex and challenging process. Getting it right all the time is pretty well impossible. However, we believe that there are certain skills and principles you can adhere to that will help you to be more effective. Good people leadership is more than simply knowing the skills; it's really all about your ability to act appropriately and to adapt your approach to suit the different people and situations you find yourself in.

> Good people leadership is more than simply knowing the skills

In our experience of working with thousands of leaders and managers in our roles as management developers and consultants, we have identified the following set of best-practice principles and we have written this book around these. The structure focuses on a range of skills, capabilities and general issues that you have to be aware of in order to be effective as a leader and manager of people in the 21st century.

We have categorised these into three key areas (see Figure 1):

▌ Focus on you – self-awareness, self-belief and self-confidence are all important for success as a leader of people. We have identified a range of areas that we believe contributes to greater self-awareness and leads to self-belief and confidence.

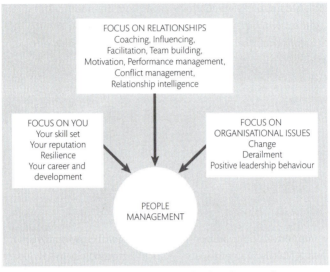

FIGURE 1 Best-practice principles for leading and managing people

▌ Focus on relationships – leading and managing people is largely about your reputation and attitudes and how you deploy your behaviour, skills and abilities when working with others. With this in mind we have identified a range of competences and capabilities, which should be part of any leader's repertoire and will contribute to your success as a leader.

▌ Focus on organisational issues – these areas concern how to lead change, avoid derailment and use positive psychology to improve results in your business area.

A brief description of these areas follows, together with a short self-reflection exercise to help you get started on the process of raising your self-awareness and planning where you may have to focus your development.

Focus on you

▮ Your skill set – being fully aware of your strengths, weaknesses and development needs.

▮ Your reputation – how others perceive you.

▮ Resilience – your ability to deal with adversity and bounce back.

▮ Your career development – having a clear sense of your personal goals and plans.

Focus on your people

▮ Coaching – developing others to help them reach their full potential.

▮ Influencing – influencing others to gain commitment and agreement to ideas and action.

▮ Facilitation – acting as an enabler, involving others to ensure good-quality dialogue and outcomes.

▮ Team building – developing and working with others to get things done for the benefit of the business.

▮ Motivation – creating a positive environment to get the best out of others.

▮ Performance management – setting goals and objectives for others and giving timely feedback.

▮ Conflict management – dealing effectively with interpersonal tensions.

▮ Relationship intelligence – managing and understanding your behaviour and emotions when working with others.

Focus on your business

▌ Change – understanding the need for, implications of and process of change.

▌ Derailment – awareness of the barriers, challenges and career derailers that could knock you off track.

▌ Positive leadership behaviour – using relational, appreciative and solution-focused approaches to lead others.

You might find it useful to complete the following self-reflection quiz, which will enable you to analyse your knowledge or skill level, your degree of self-awareness and your development needs in the main areas covered in this book. If you want to get even more valuable feedback you might like to ask others – your boss and colleagues – to rate you against these criteria as well. (Please feel free to photocopy this quiz should you wish to get feedback from others.)

Using a scale of 1–7, try rating yourself in relation to each of the main people leadership areas: 1 = a low level of skill, 4 = a satisfactory skill level and 7 = you are highly skilled in this area. Then indicate development need in relation to your current role and future development.

Self-reflection quiz

People management self-reflection quiz		
People leadership areas	**Skill/knowledge level** 1-----4-------7	**Development need:** Low/Med/High
Your skill set – being fully aware of your strengths, weaknesses and development needs		
Your reputation – how others perceive you		
Resilience – your ability to deal with adversity and bounce back		
Your career development – having a clear sense of your personal goals and plans		
Coaching – developing others to help them reach their full potential		
Influencing – influencing others to gain commitment and agreement to ideas and action		
Facilitation – acting as an enabler, involving others to ensure good-quality dialogue and outcomes		
Team building – developing and working with others to get things done for the benefit of the business		

People leadership areas	Skill/knowledge level 1-----4-------7	Development need: Low/Med/High
Motivation – creating a positive environment to get the best out of others		
Performance management – setting goals and objectives for others and giving timely feedback		
Conflict management – dealing effectively with interpersonal tensions		
Relationship intelligence – managing and understanding behaviour and emotions when working with others		
Change – understanding the need for and implications of change and delivering successful outcomes		
Derailment – awareness of the barriers, challenges and career derailers that could knock you off track		
Positive leadership behaviour – using relational, appreciative and solution-focused processes to lead others		

NOTES

The remainder of this book will focus on each of the areas described above and will share best-practice ideas, tips and techniques together with practical work to help you develop your skill and capability as a leader.

This book can be read either in a conventional way, from beginning to end, or by dipping in and out, reading the sections that are of most interest and use to you. You will find that we have incorporated several quizzes, inventories and exercises into the various chapters. These are intended as a way of encouraging you to reflect, learn and create action plans for further development.

You

Your reputation

It takes 20 years to build a reputation and five minutes to ruin it. If you think about that, you'll do things differently.

Warren Buffett, investment guru

When managing and leading people, your reputation becomes a critical factor. What do we mean by reputation? It is essentially a collective system of subjective beliefs among members of a social group. It's about how others judge or evaluate us. Our reputation affects our behaviour in that we will tend to behave in certain ways in order to develop, maintain and protect our reputation.

It doesn't matter what level of leader or manager you are, your reputation is created through all of your actions and interactions and will have an impact upon your credibility, effectiveness and success. Managing and building your reputation takes care and consideration. It is multi-faceted and will be based upon your values and beliefs and how these play out in the way you manage yourself and your relationships in life. It is dynamic and will fluctuate over time according to circumstances and how others know and perceive you as an individual. It is built over a long time period and will be developed by both your own actions and how others observe and experience you.

Managing and building your reputation takes care and consideration

Lots of work goes into earning a good reputation, yet it can be damaged or even destroyed in seconds. There have been many examples of this over recent years, at both an organisation and an individual level, for example in the banking industry, in politics and sports. And these are only the examples in the public eye. There are numerous day-to-day examples of managers and leaders who risk their reputation by careless behaviour towards others. Reputation is not necessarily about being liked, it's more about being respected and trusted.

Components of reputation

So how can you build and develop your reputation? We believe it's about paying attention to certain principles and values, then demonstrating these in your day-to-day life. These are shown in Figure 1.1.

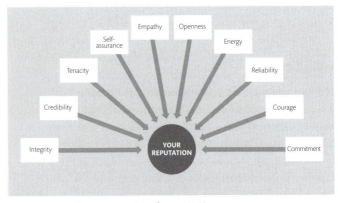

FIGURE 1.1 Components of reputation

Integrity

This involves demonstrating honesty and strong moral principles. It's about being honest with both yourself and others and behaving consistently in ways that align with your personal moral code. Integrity is often defined as doing the right thing for the right reasons at the right time. In order to behave with integrity you must identify your moral code, which is determined by a set of principles and values that you decide is important for you to live a satisfying and rewarding life.

When considering this area of your reputation you might like to reflect on the past and the decisions and choices you have made in life. In thinking about how you have managed your life so far, you can begin to identify the principles and rules you apply to your behaviour in different settings, and then begin to assess your level of personal integrity. You may also identify your weak spots and the barriers that you should overcome in order to further develop your reputation and personal integrity.

As Warren Buffett, the successful investor and CEO of Berkshire Hathaway, says: 'In looking for people to hire, you look for three qualities: integrity, intelligence, and energy. And if they don't have the first, the other two will kill you.'

Credibility

This is associated with your expertise, your credentials and your confidence. Having a sound track record of good judgement, giving examples of your experience and successes, demonstrating your knowledge and expertise will all contribute to your personal credibility. But this credibility can also be built by the way you relate to others, for instance:

- your non-verbal behaviours, such as eye contact
- vocal usage, such as articulacy, which contributes to self-confidence
- demonstrating shared values by making connections and associations
- building rapport
- following through on commitments
- admitting your mistakes
- keeping confidences
- giving credit to others
- asking for and giving feedback.

It is worth taking time to reflect on your level of credibility in the organisation. Having high personal credibility will enable you to gain legitimacy as a leader and manager who is respected, trusted and supported by others.

Tenacity

This is about persistence, showing determination, not giving up and sticking with it when things get tough. Being tenacious can make the difference between mediocrity and greatness. It is about purpose, drive, resilience and willpower. When you have a purpose in life you have a goal to aim for, with milestones, priorities, plans to be met. Each of us will undoubtedly encounter challenges, barriers and setbacks in our lives. Those who demonstrate tenacity will stick with their dreams and learn from these challenges and often come back stronger. Largely, tenacity is about self-belief and ability to meet your goals. It's not difficult to develop – it's about drive and persistence.

> Tenacity is about self-belief and ability to meet your goals

You might like to reflect on challenges you have faced in your life, perhaps those that have involved a setback. Ask yourself how you overcame these and how you got back on track.

Self-assurance

This is about being poised, self-reliant and sure of yourself, showing composure and coolness even when under pressure. Of course, we all experience situations where our self-assuredness is challenged. Typically this happens at times when we are not in control, for instance when speaking in public or being interviewed by the press. The secret here is to focus on our strengths and think positively. Preparation, planning and rehearsal for those events and situations that we know make us nervous will help. So it's worthwhile thinking about the types of situations and events where you demonstrate self-assuredness and those where you feel nervous or lacking in self-assurance.

Empathy

This is about understanding other people's points of view, sharing the feelings of others and seeing situations through their eyes. People who demonstrate empathy recognise that it is important to consider the other person's point of view as well as their perception of us. Empathy is not about always agreeing with others, nor is it about giving in – it's about seeing things from the other person's perspective and then showing them that you have done so. For example, when discussing an issue where there is disagreement and emotions are running high, you can demonstrate empathy by saying something like: *'I understand your concern about this issue, Pablo, and I can see how it might affect you. Can you just tell me a little more about where your concerns come from?'*

In order to reflect on your personal skill in this area it is worth considering how often you get negative reactions from people or how often people stop listening or show lack of interest in what you are saying. These are real indicators that you may not be demonstrating empathy towards others.

Openness

This involves approachability and a willingness to be receptive to ideas, opinions, behaviours, cultures and experiences that are not your own. People who demonstrate this skill are curious, deal well with ambiguity and enjoy experiencing new situations and possibilities. They have a genuine inquisitiveness, ask lots of questions and show interest in others' experiences. They often express appreciation and willingness to take part in new projects or experiences, thus demonstrating an authentic desire to try new and unfamiliar things. This indicates to others their interest and disposition to challenge the status quo when necessary. The real definition of openness is about not being closed to others' ideas and viewpoints and being willing to look at things from a different perspective and change if necessary.

Energy

This is about having enthusiasm and vitality and demonstrating this to others. It is being motivated and passionate about your job, your organisation, your product or your project. If you can't demonstrate motivation and energy for whatever you are involved in, how can you expect others to engage with it? In some ways energy is not measurable, but it is noticed and read by the people around us. It is often the simple things that demonstrate energy, for instance:

▌ your facial expression – eye contact, smile

▌ your voice – varied intonation, pace, pitch

▌ your gestures – are they supportive and appropriate?

▌ your language – is it emotional and logical?

▌ your emotions – are you able to demonstrate your emotions in your actions?

It is often the simple things that demonstrate energy

Reliability

This is the quality of being dependable and trustworthy. Reliability is one of the key components necessary to build trust. The first step in the reliability component is being consistent and accountable. This involves setting yourself realistic goals that are achievable, meeting your commitments and consistently delivering good performance. In relation to others, it means that you communicate clearly, fulfil your promises and support your people. People will find you reliable when you show dedication, timeliness and accountability in all aspects of your work and fulfil commitments to work colleagues. Reliable people create a sense of security and support in the working environment that enables people to operate in an effective and efficient manner. In essence, it means that others believe they can count on you.

Courage

This is at the heart of successful leadership. It is about demonstrating strength in the face of adversity and being able to stand up for what is right when faced with a difficult situation and then being able to see things through to the end. Courageous people take full responsibility for their words and actions and are not afraid to admit their mistakes. Courage involves:

▌ using your initiative

▌ taking action

▌ speaking up for what you believe

▌ challenging the status quo when necessary

▌ leading and implementing change

▌ making and taking both popular and unpopular decisions

▌ asking for and giving feedback

▌ facing up to and dealing with conflict.

Courageous people will overcome any fear they may feel by dealing with challenges, obstacles and adversity with confidence and conviction.

> Courageous people take full responsibility for their words and actions

Commitment

This is about demonstrating loyalty and fulfilling one's obligations. Commitment to yourself, your colleagues, your organisation, your profession and your passions is important here. It's about 'walking the talk', having a sound set of beliefs and values that you regularly demonstrate in the way you live your life both at and outside work. It is about ensuring that your actions and words are aligned. Showing that you are accountable for your actions, displaying care and concern for others and generally appreciating others' contributions by saying more than a simple thank you will help to contribute to your overall reputation as a good leader. (Our list is not exhaustive and you may find there are other components that are relevant to your particular situation.)

You may now like to evaluate yourself in relation to these elements that we believe contribute to reputation development.

Exercise

Using the following assessment tool, indicate where you believe you currently sit on the spectrum. Use the scale 1–10, where 1 is 'this does not relate to me' and 10 is 'this is very like me', and give an example for each element in relation to your reputation as a leader or manager.

Personal reputation assessment tool
Integrity
1_____5_____10
Credibility
1_____5_____10
Tenacity
1_____5_____10
Self-assurance
1_____5_____10

Personal reputation assessment tool

Empathy
1_____5_____10

Openness
1_____5_____10

Energy
1_____5_____10

Reliability
1_____5_____10

Courage
1_____5_____10

Commitment
1_____5_____10

Add and evaluate any other principles that you believe to be important to creating and managing your reputation.

Once you have completed this short self-assessment you may like to use the information to check out your views against those of others. You could ask your boss, colleagues or direct reports to complete the assessment in relation to their views about you. Alternatively, you could be more selective and focus on only a few of the principles, perhaps those that you feel less certain about or where you have a low score.

When you have identified the areas where you need to develop it is important to have an action plan detailing specific steps. Once you have done this, give yourself a month or so using the new behaviours and then score yourself again. For instance, let's say you rate yourself low in the empathy principle. You may like to think about how you could demonstrate more empathy with your colleagues by listening to their needs, observing their moods and behaviours and asking them questions to show you are interested and empathetic. In addition to this action plan you must reassess your skill and the best way of doing this is to get feedback from someone you trust.

These principles and values are about attitude, behaviour and capability. In order to ensure that you develop and maintain a positive reputation, where trust and respect are key features, you should pay attention to how you conduct yourself with the people in your relationship network. How you demonstrate these components of reputation and how others perceive them will contribute to how people regard you as an individual.

> *'The way to gain a good reputation is to endeavour to be what you desire to appear.'*
>
> Socrates

But how do you know about your reputation and how others regard you? First of all you must be clear with yourself about how you wish to be perceived and which personal values and beliefs you feel are important to you. Getting feedback from others, either formally or informally, will help you to confirm how you are regarded. This can be done in the following ways:

▌ *Asking others for feedback.* Create a feedback culture with your colleagues by regularly asking questions about your performance and introducing opportunities for everyone to offer each other feedback. If you start by asking people to give appreciative feedback, this can make them feel more relaxed about giving feedback, which can then be developed further by incorporating developmental feedback which will help individuals to grow even further. Creating a feedback culture will help establish and develop a trusting, respectful and vibrant working environment.

▌ *Taking part in formal 360-degree feedback processes.*
These are often offered as part of management
development courses or as part of an organisation's
performance management process.

▌ *Honing your reputation antennae.* Are you someone
people choose to work with and involve in their projects?
Do people come to you for advice, information and
encouragement? Do people value your opinion and listen
to you?

> You must be clear with yourself about
> how you wish to be perceived

Understanding and knowing how others perceive you
will enable you to actively manage and develop your
reputation to ensure that it fits with your values, beliefs
and needs.

It is also important to recognise that your reputation depends
upon value judgements and perceptions of others, and as
these can change over time you must always be actively
managing your behaviour to ensure you maintain a positive
reputation.

Tips for success

▌ Think about what you stand for. What is important to
you?

▌ Have a clear and realistic idea of how other people
perceive you.

▌ Seek feedback from others.

▌ Make sure you act on any feedback you receive.

▌ Conduct regular 'reputation audits' like the one above.

▌ Make sure your words and actions are congruent.

▌ Remember that reputation can take years to build but can
be destroyed in seconds.

Your career

If one does not know to which port one is sailing, no wind is favourable.

Seneca, Roman philosopher

In the past you may have been able to depend upon an organisation to plan and support your development, but in today's fast-moving, ever-changing and far less secure world it would be irresponsible not to recognise that your development, career and life plans are your responsibility, and yours alone. There are many people who can and will support you in your endeavours, but in the end it is up to you to map out your personal development plans, career development plans and life plans.

As a leader of people it is your responsibility not only to take control of your career and development but to help others do the same. Acting as a role model in this area by actively taking control and demonstrating how you manage your career and development will enhance your credibility and reputation as a leader.

One of the questions we ask managers on our programmes and when conducting research interviews is: 'What do you wish you'd known earlier in order to help your career development?' Many of the most popular answers relate to personal development, career development and life planning. People very often mention:

- recognise opportunities and take them
- be more open to taking unexpected routes in your career
- be prepared to follow your dreams (Steve Jobs talks about this in one of the TED talks he delivered, 'How to live before you die'. You might like to view it at **www.TED.com/talks/steve_jobs_how_to_live_before_you_die.html**)
- map out what you want out of life at an early stage
- recognise the importance of continuous learning
- get to grips with managing people early in a career
- leave time for life
- be prepared to step out of a comfort zone
- set boundaries: work–life balance is important
- put personal development at the top of any priority list
- seek out opportunities to develop and grow
- take a few more risks – calculated ones, of course.

Most of us spend insufficient time thinking about our personal development plans, let alone our career development and life plans. People who do so are more likely to be committed, more focused and more likely to fulfil their ambitions. Creating strategies for success in your life, career and personal development will help you achieve your objectives.

There are many ways to take charge of your life and make the most of your potential. We believe that having goals and a structure will help. Most of the managers we talk to wish they had spent more time reflecting on, thinking through and planning their career journey – not in an obsessive way, but more as a strategy to follow and to help make decisions about the milestones in their career journey and the personal development necessary to fulfil dreams, ambitions and goals.

Self-reflection

Figure 2.1 illustrates the typical milestones you may face in your life and career.

FIGURE 2.1 Life/career milestones

Together with these milestones we have found that the process suggested in Figure 2.2 is a good starting point to being more organised and focused in this area.

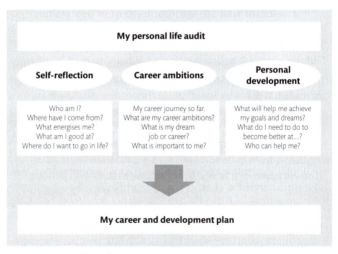

FIGURE 2.2 Self-reflection

There are five key questions to get you started on the self-reflection process, which will help you navigate your way through the many decisions you may have to make:

▌ Who am I?

▌ Where have I come from?

▌ What energises me?

▌ What am I good at?

▌ Where do I want to get to in life?

One way of dealing with these questions is to undertake a personal audit by creating a biography which tracks your life so far and helps you to picture your life ahead. Reflecting helps you to understand who you are, how you got to where you are today and to begin to plan for the future. Areas to consider for inclusion in your biography are:

▌ date of birth

▌ position in family:

– eldest, in the middle or youngest?

▌ parents' jobs

▌ siblings' jobs

▌ education and development:

– schools, college, university, professional qualifications

▌ memorable moments, achievements, disappointments

▌ management development or skill development programmes undertaken and their usefulness

▌ any feedback you have received from personality- or competence-based inventories or questionnaires – what do these tell you?

▌ career history and transitions:

– reflect on how long you stayed in each role

– what caused you to move on?

– in each case, what you found most enjoyable about the job

– how your role added/adds value to the organisation

    – memorable moments, achievements and
      disappointments

▎ how would you describe your values? Make a list of those
   things that are most important to you

▎ what energises you?

▎ what do you think you are naturally good at?

▎ what do you think you are not good at?

▎ key achievements in your life so far

▎ disappointments in your life so far

▎ hobbies and interests

▎ favourite books, movies, songs.

Reflecting helps you to understand who you are

You may find it useful to copy the following chart to record
this information.

My personal biography	
Family information	
Date of birth: Position in family:	Parents' occupations: Mother: Father: Siblings' occupations:

Education and development	
Formal education	**Personal and management development**
Schools attended:	Short courses attended:
Further education:	Personality/competence/ inventories completed:
Qualification attained:	

Reflections
Memorable moments, achievements, disappointments and any feedback you have had from education and development:

Career history and transitions
Starting with your first job, list your job title/s, organisations worked for and time with each one. In each case also indicate what you found most enjoyable about the job and what caused you to move on.

Career highs and lows
Reflect on all your jobs and the organisations you have worked for and identify memorable moments, achievements and disappointments.

Memorable moments	Achievements	Disappointments

Summary
Look back over your biography so far and summarise by asking yourself the following questions and noting your responses:

What energises you in a job?

What saps your energy?

What are you naturally good at?

What are you not good at?

Identify your main achievements in life so far:

Identify any disappointments in your life so far:

NOTES

It is important for you to personalise this audit and make it your own, so the areas above are simply suggestions for reflection. You should structure it in a way that best suits you. One popular way of recording your thoughts is to create a life audit diary (you could, of course, create your own version of this on your computer) where you keep notes and plans which enable you to structure thoughts and make notes on your reflections. Be creative, use mind maps and other imagery to help make plans and develop ideas about your development, career and life in general. Having a journal where you record your thoughts and ideas enables you to reflect over the years to see patterns, progress and generally track your development, career and life journey.

> Be creative, use mind maps and other imagery to help make plans

Ideally this is something you should do on an occasional basis throughout your life. Each of us works to different timescales – we find that reflecting every two to five years helps us to focus, keep on track and reorient as necessary. It is important to recognise that plans and ideas have to be adaptable as things change throughout one's life. Getting used to a reflective process and keeping notes will help you to adapt, reorient and plan when necessary.

George Bernard Shaw said: '*Life isn't about finding yourself. Life is about creating yourself.*' The problem is that many people do not take control and navigate their own journey; most simply allow things to happen to them. While this may mean things turn out well, we believe that each of us has a duty to take control of our own life and career and to help others do the same. Our research indicates that people who take responsibility are much more likely to be motivated by their choices and are better performers because of this.

Each time you reflect on your life, you must also begin the process of looking to the future. So, the next question to ask yourself is: '*Where do I want to get to?*' This is a complex question and will undoubtedly change over time, but the important thing is to think big, dream and let your imagination be free. We will all have a unique way of answering this question – some of this will depend upon the life and career stage you find yourself at. It's a question we often ask people when coaching them – no one finds it easy to answer. Here are some of the answers we have received:

▌ '*So far I've had a pretty successful career. I am approaching 50, the kids are all off making lives for themselves, and my wife and I are now looking towards our future. Ideally I'd like to make one more career move, to director level, see a bit more of the world – I've always wanted to visit China – and invest more time in keeping fit and healthy.*' (John was a marketing manager in a FTSE 100 company, he enjoyed his job and decided to have executive coaching to help him plan for his next career move.)

▌ '*I want to be retired by the time I am 45, having set up, run and sold my own successful IT company.*' (Khaleef was a 32-year-old IT specialist who attended a Leadership Programme at Ashridge. He worked for a small start-up company, was very focused, had a clear career plan and admitted to being a workaholic. His challenge was to think more broadly about life in general and he became more aware of this through the coaching sessions.)

'That's the problem, I don't know. After I graduated I took a job with the bank and have worked my way up the career ladder in a logical way. I don't hate my job, but then it's not exactly what I dreamed I'd be doing when I started university. What I do know is that I want to get out of this organisation and begin to do something that excites and challenges me. Other aspects of my life are pretty good – my husband and I would like to start a family and I keep myself fit, though sometimes work gets in the way, so making sure I have better work–life balance is important.' (Siobhan then went on to tell me that this was why she had joined the women's mentoring programme. She realised that she needed help to reflect, plan and look ahead more purposefully.)

So, how will you answer this question and what are the implications for the rest of your career?

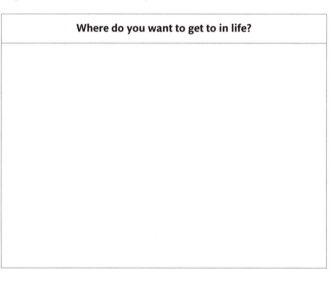

Where do you want to get to in life?

Focus on career future

The next stage in the process is to focus in detail on your career, and most importantly, what your career ambitions are, so that you can plan how to achieve them. In the previous stage you looked back over your career; now the challenge is to draw lessons from previous reflections, learn from your current situation and plan ahead for the next steps and beyond.

So, careerwise, where do you see yourself going in the future and how are you going to get there? Luck will play a role in managing your career, of course. However, if you don't know what's important to you and what your career ambitions are, even luck won't help.

> Luck will play a role in managing your career

One way of identifying what is important to you is to explore your values. Values are those beliefs we hold about the things in life that are important to us and therefore have an influence over the choices we make and the behaviour we use. Our values are influenced by many things, but predominantly by our upbringing, home life, education, religion, work life, family, friends and in general the social environment and context we live in. Identifying the values that you hold dear can help to inform your career future, as people prefer to build a career based on those things that are important to them. Of course, values can and do change over time and are often affected by the career and life stage you are at. So this is an exercise worth doing at all the different stages. Some values may stay with you all through your life, while others may become important at different stages in your life.

So, have a look at Table 2.1 and select those values that you regard as important for you in your career.

TABLE 2.1 Values selector

Ambition	Determination	Independence	Equality	Discretion
Freedom	Humility	Spirituality	Commitment	Fun
Creativity	Loyalty	Curiosity	Optimism	Duty
Honesty	Work–life balance	Social responsibility	Competence	Humour
Respect	Fairness	Teamwork	Tolerance	Responsibility
Integrity	Compassion	Accountability	Courage	Self-control

Value summary

List the top 12 values that you regard as important for your career – use the list above as a starter, but it is best to define your own values.

This exercise should help you to begin the focusing process and enable you to more clearly understand those values and beliefs that inform your career choice.

Reflecting on your current job is also a worthwhile part of the process. Think about the various elements of your role and how these are contributing to your success, development and future dreams and ambitions. One way of doing this is to create a job tree, which is a graphic way of summarising your objectives and the key elements of your job. Figure 2.3 (overleaf) shows a sample job tree for the role of tutor at Ashridge Business School.

This basic job tree is constructed by taking a blank sheet of paper (we find A3 size is best), drawing a tree trunk onto it and annotating it with your job title. Start creating your tree by adding branches, which represent the main elements of

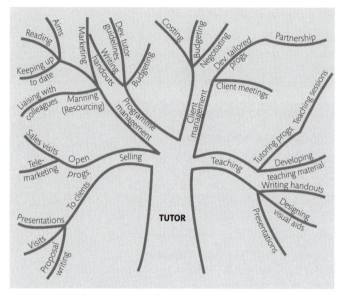

FIGURE 2.3 Job tree example

your job (usually about 6–8), and annotate them accordingly (line management, business development, administration, etc.). Now take each branch or element in turn and add smaller branches (or twigs), annotating them as you go to describe the tasks you do on a day-to-day basis within each element. This process is best done over a few hours and even left overnight to enable you to remember the detail of your job.

Once you have this basic job tree, the next stage is to use this data to analyse your job and draw lessons from this analysis that will help you to make decisions about your career and development. So, ask yourself the following questions and make notes onto your tree:

▌ How much time do you spend on each of the main elements of your role? Indicate this by percentage for each element.

▌ Which elements and tasks energise and give you
satisfaction?

▌ Which elements and tasks do you dislike?

Rate each of the elements in relation to:

▌ its importance to your success in the organisation

▌ your skill and ability

▌ where you feel you need to develop.

The purpose of the job tree is to provide you with a
graphical image representing a full analysis of your current
job. The next stage in this process is to begin to draw
meaning from your analysis that will help you to plan your
way ahead in relation to your career and development.

This sort of analysis should help you to understand more
about what it is you seek in a job and career. Your challenge
now is to set yourself goals and objectives for managing your
career future. Use the box below to write down your three
key goals. Once you have these goals and objectives you can
begin the final stage of the process, which is to plan your
development in order to help you fulfil these ambitions.

My career future Goals and objectives
Goal 1
Goal 2
Goal 3

Focus on my personal development

The last stage of the process is where you begin to plan your future development. It is about assimilating all the information you have gathered from your review so far into a plan that summarises:

▌ what will help you achieve your goals and dreams

▌ what you need to do specifically to become better at each of your goals

▌ who can help you

▌ how you will measure success.

One way of doing this is to create an action plan for each of your goals in your life audit diary. At this stage it is important to be realistic – realistic in terms of the number of goals, how you can put plans in place to achieve them, who will help you and the timing.

You might find the following action planning log useful. You should use one of these logs for each of your goals.

Goal	
Action	**Timescale**
People who can help me	
How success will be measured	

The purpose of this process is to help you to take control and responsibility for your life, career and development. As we suggested earlier, managers who take control are more

likely to achieve their ambitions, to enjoy their work and to
perform to a high standard.

> ## Managers who take control are more likely to achieve their ambitions

As a manager it is also incumbent upon you to share these
ideas and processes with your team. In Chapter 4 we talk
about the manager's role as a coach. The ideas introduced
in this chapter are ones you can easily incorporate into
coaching sessions and share with others to encourage them
to take responsibility for and control over their life, career
and development.

Tips for success

▌ Take control of your career – don't assume others will.

▌ Create a career and development plan.

▌ Recognise the importance of continuous learning.

▌ Seek out opportunities to develop and grow.

▌ Make self-reflection a regular part of your routine.

▌ Keep your focus on the big picture rather than allowing
   yourself to be bogged down with details.

Your resilience

A good half of the art of living is resilience.

Alain de Botton, philosopher and writer

Resilience is the ability to speedily recover from adverse events and bounce back to our normal behaviour. There are many examples of people who demonstrate this characteristic on a day-to-day basis – for instance, the person who contracts a life-threatening disease and deals with it with dignity and grace and becomes stronger as a result; the soldier who loses a limb in war and goes on to run a marathon; the manager who is made redundant after 20-plus years' service with an organisation and goes on to set up their own successful business. If we all put our minds to it we can think of several people in our own relationship network that we would describe as resilient.

Resilience isn't just about bouncing back from life-changing events, it's also about being able to deal with the smaller day-to-day pressures and challenges that are part of your routine work. Nor is it about not experiencing pain, disappointment or failure. Any truly resilient person will tell you they have experienced all these emotions and many more, and the real skill is in how you deal with these situations and learn from them. A person's ability to cope with setbacks, challenges and day-to-day problems and move

on while also sustaining good-quality performance is largely
what resilience is all about.

Our focus in this chapter will be on resilience in relation to
day-to-day pressures and challenges. While people need both
kinds of resilience, we believe that understanding how you
react to and cope with challenges and pressures will enable
you to learn more about your personal resilience and how
you can further develop this for even greater effectiveness.
Most of us have demonstrated resilience at some point in
our lives, and many experts in this area suggest that being
resilient is quite common. Our intent is to encourage you to
think about how you cope with setbacks and challenges, to
identify the features of resilient behaviour, to help you think
through how you can be more resilient, and how you can
help others develop their skill and capability in this area.

> Most of us have demonstrated resilience
> at some point in our lives

Features of resilience

Our colleague, Alex Davda, has researched this area and
developed the Ashridge Resilience Questionnaire, which is
designed to help you take stock of your personal resilience
and to develop it even further. Alex has identified a range
of attitudes that he believes contributes to an individual's
level of resilience. We have adapted his ideas and developed
them further into what we consider to be a range of features
that you need to be aware of as contributing to your personal
resilience.

Each one of us will undoubtedly face many issues which
will test our resilience, for instance:

▌ redundancy

▌ personality clashes

▌ deadlines

▌ bullying

▌ relocation

▌ demanding clients

▌ personal tragedy.

You might like to reflect on a recent setback, challenge or even a crisis in your life that you believe you have overcome and bounced back from. Reflect on the situation and the period afterwards and think about the way you dealt with it, your behaviour, your feelings, who helped and in general how you coped. Make notes about this and use it to reflect on your general ability to 'bounce back'. Then reflect on other challenges to determine whether or not a pattern is emerging that you can learn from. It is worth mentioning

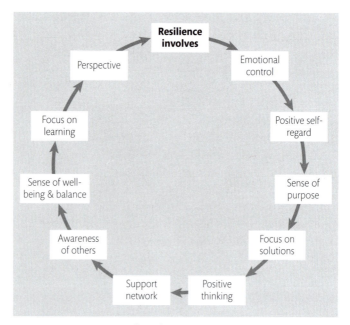

FIGURE 3.1 Features of resilience

that any setbacks or pressures in your personal life will also affect resilience at work.

Everyone can develop further in the area of personal resilience. The ideas in Figure 3.1 may be useful for you as well as for helping others to understand this important area.

In looking at each of these key features we try to illustrate how these features can apply in reality.

Emotional control

This starts with you being able to understand what you are feeling at any given time and why. Having the ability to name your emotions (even if only to yourself) is a good starting point. Naming and understanding your emotions makes it easier to manage them in a positive and productive way. It is also worth considering what it is that triggers both appropriate and inappropriate responses. This level of self-awareness will help you to recognise when control and moderation are necessary and when it is appropriate to show emotion. Emotional control and awareness will help you to understand more about the reactions you have to certain issues and ultimately to select appropriate behaviour in order to deal effectively with even the most challenging situations.

Positive self-regard

This is about your overall sense of personal value and self-esteem. Being self-confident involves having a positive view of yourself, an awareness of your strengths, capabilities and accomplishments, and sense of trust in your instincts. People who have positive self-belief are typically far more resilient than those who lack this trait. Of course, you must beware that this self-regard is not overdone and therefore turns into arrogance.

Being self-confident involves having a positive view of yourself

Having a positive self-regard implies that you have a coping mechanism for dealing with many of the challenges that life throws at you. People with self-belief tend to recognise that life is a roller-coaster. When faced with adversity your ability to work through the situation, accept failure and occasional unhappiness means that you will develop your own coping mechanisms to help you manage your way through.

Sense of purpose

This is about having meaning in your life. It gives your life focus and helps you understand what and who is important to you. Knowing what it is that motivates and energises you in life will help keep you on track in times of adversity. People who have a sense of purpose have focus and control in their lives. It helps you to concentrate on the future and your way ahead. Purpose gives your life meaning and will help you deal with day-to-day challenges and encounters. So, do you know what your purpose is in life? Reflect for a moment here and write down some thoughts.

Focus on solutions

People deal with problems in different ways. We believe that by adopting a solution focus to problems and challenges you are more likely to place your emphasis on what is possible and within your control to change and therefore move forward, often in small steps, but nonetheless the movement demonstrates resilience. So, for instance, if you are faced with a major challenge such as a colleague who is making life difficult for you, try this process. Ask yourself what the quality of your relationship is on a scale of 1 to 10 (1 being low and 10 being high). Then ask yourself what level you would like to be at for the relationship to be more valuable. Think about small steps that you could take to move in the right direction. By focusing on solutions in small steps you are more likely to move forward successfully. For more on solution-focus approaches, see Chapter 14).

> Think about small steps that you could take to move in the right direction

Positive thinking

This is about developing an optimistic approach to life. Being a positive thinker is not about being unrealistic, rather it is about seeking to focus on what is possible in any situation and recognising that positive thinking is a more energetic and healthy way of looking at the world that will lead to positive outcomes. Demonstrating positive thinking means that you project a can-do attitude, which is one of the key skills of resilience.

Support network

Knowing who is in your support network and who you can ask for help in times of crisis is vital. It is rare to find someone who can overcome adversity without support from others. So, take time to build and nurture your networks and understand what help each of the people in your network can offer. It is especially useful to develop mutually supportive relationships where you can be sounding boards, devil's advocates and provide reassurance to each other when necessary. As the old saying goes, 'a problem shared is a problem halved'. However, simply sharing isn't enough, you must develop relationships with those people who will actively work with you, people you trust and respect as valuable colleagues. Sometimes simply getting a different perspective on a problem can enable you to look at it with new eyes and so adopt a process that will help you move forward. You might find it useful to make a note of the people in your support network.

Awareness of others

This is about having the ability to empathise with and understand others by asking them how they are managing during challenging situations. You need to pay attention to the people who are dealing well with the situation as well as those who are demonstrating less positive reactions. As a boss or colleague, being aware of others' emotional and behavioural changes will help give you perspective about how you and others deal with challenges and setbacks. This awareness will not only be beneficial to your personal resilience but will also help you to build your reputation as a supportive and effective leader.

Sense of well-being and balance

Well-being is defined in many different ways and can mean different things to different people. For instance:

▌ social well-being is about having good quality relationships

▌ physical well-being is about fitness and health

▌ financial well-being is about reward and security

▌ spiritual well-being in the context of work might mean doing work that is of value and has purpose.

In addition, many people talk about having balance in their life. Understanding what contributes to your feelings of well-being will support you through adversity. Recognising how you maintain balance and what you do to maintain your overall health and energy for life will affect the way you deal with stress and pressure. Develop coping techniques by knowing when to change gear and take time out of the stressful situation to recharge your batteries – for instance, by taking exercise, having a coffee and stretch break, finding a friend to take a walk with or simply doing something different.

> Develop coping techniques by knowing when to change gear

Focus on learning

This is about being open-minded, interested in developing and learning new skills, and constantly seeking opportunities to explore new ideas, which will all contribute to your ability to deal with stressful and challenging situations. Such situations often provide exciting learning opportunities. What you are experiencing as challenge or stress may simply be that you are being pushed out of your comfort zone. By being open to new ideas and willing to learn new skills and ways of doing things, you will find that situations that were previously stressful turn into learning opportunities. Of course, this sounds easy, but it will often demand a change of attitude and disposition towards the unknown.

Perspective

Resilience can be affected by the perspective you take on any situation. It is therefore important to understand what it is that triggers your feelings of pressure, stress or challenge. Once you know this you can then evaluate your understanding of these situations. When you take a step back and explore your perspective, things seem less stressful than first anticipated, and by slowing down, focusing and exploring your perspective you can apply some of the approaches above to help you deal with the situation.

We all deal with stress and pressure in different ways – some people thrive when working in pressurised situations, whereas others will wilt. Some people are naturally resilient, but all of us can improve our level of resilience. One of the keys is to know what it is that causes you most stress and pressure. Once you are aware of your stressors it is easier to develop coping mechanisms by deploying some of the tactics and approaches described above.

In order to raise your awareness of your levels of resilience you may like to complete the following quiz, which could help you to identify those areas where you are most vulnerable and how you currently cope with pressure and stress.

All of us can improve our level of resilience

Looking at the results of your quiz, if you have answered mostly 'Yes' then you are quite resilient already, if mostly 'To some extent' then you are on the right track, and if mostly 'No' it suggests that your resilience is quite weak and you are therefore vulnerable and need to work on your skills and capabilities. Having completed the quiz, and in order to develop your levels of resilience, you may like to reflect on your answers and select two or three areas where you believe you are vulnerable, and focus on developing these. For instance, if you feel you do not find it easy to turn off and relax, it may be worth identifying ways of improving this – perhaps by going for a walk, practising yoga, listening

Personal resilience quiz				
Question	Yes	To some extent	No	Notes
1. I feel confident in my skills and beliefs				
2. I adapt to change and uncertainty				
3. I feel in control of my emotional reactions				
4. I feel energetic and in control of my work–life balance				
5. I recover quickly from setbacks				
6. I have goals and focus in my life				
7. I find it easy to empathise with others				
8. I find it easy to turn off and relax				
9. I have a good support network in place				
10. I take an optimistic approach to most things				
Totals				

to music, reading a good book. The key is to identify what works for you. You may also like to think about the long term and identify any life strategies that you can put in place. It may be useful here to sit down with a friend and work through some of the issues.

Part of your role as a leader involves helping others to develop their resilience. Typically, resilient people are more reliable, more optimistic and maintain a higher level of performance overall. So, you should encourage others to examine what stresses and challenges them and maybe encourage them to complete the quiz above as a starting point to help them understand how they can develop their levels of resilience.

Tips for success

As an individual:

▌ Identify your main stressors.

▌ Think about a time when you have bounced back from a setback and identify what it was that you did. How can you learn from that experience?

▌ When you feel pressure or stress, focus on your emotional response – try to name the emotions you feel and why you feel that way. This can lead to greater emotional control and self-awareness.

▌ Be aware of the coping mechanisms you currently deploy and develop new ones.

▌ Be prepared to ask for help.

As a manager:

▌ Observe others and help them recognise their stressors.

▌ Be aware of people's levels of resilience and the differences between people.

▌Pay attention to how people are coping and identify those who have coping mechanisms and those who put on a brave face.

▌Be prepared to help others to develop resilience and coping mechanisms.

part

2

Your people

Coaching

In research conducted over the past three years we've found that leaders who have the best coaching skills have better business results.

VP of Global Executive and Organisational Development at IBM

The art of coaching and delegation is an essential part of the effective people leader's toolkit. So, what do we mean by coaching? Coaching is largely about listening to the other person and helping them to improve their effectiveness. There are a number of definitions of coaching, but for us it is about enabling people to think for themselves and come up with their own options and possibilities, rather than telling people what to do or just giving advice. Delegation is often associated with the coaching process. When done well it involves allowing your colleagues to develop their skills and knowledge to their full potential.

Why coach?

There are a number of reasons to encourage a coaching climate in your organisation. It is also important for you to develop your skills in this area.

▌ *People need to learn continually.* Learning is important. When products and services are similar, competitive advantage comes from having people with ideas, skills, responsibility and initiative. The core idea of coaching is to develop others, to help them learn. Without coaching this cannot be achieved. Ultimately, as the environment grows more and more complex, performance will be as a result of learning. To paraphrase Reg Revans, the founder of Action Learning, if the environment changes faster than your organisation learns, you're out of business. Jack Welch of GE has also made this phrase his own. This means that we cannot wait for the rest of the organisation to change before we change – we have to take individual responsibility for learning, and as a people manager, encourage others to do the same.

▌ *To help people.* Ultimately effective coaching is about helping people to achieve something they want to achieve, whether it is promotion, skills, improved performance, self-understanding or better balance. Coaching has to focus primarily on the individual being coached, in conjunction with the needs of the organisation.

▌ *To give others responsibility and ownership.* The main aim of coaching is about better performance, whatever the field of coaching: sport, the arts or business. People perform better when they take responsibility and ownership for their actions. They can't do that if you are micro-managing them.

▌ *To develop your skills as a leader.* Leadership entails taking a step back from the operational details of the job and looking more at the strategic and human elements. You won't be able to accomplish this if you are busy doing everything. Practising the art of coaching will help you to become an effective leader.

▌ *To get people to think for themselves and develop initiative.* If you are the person who ends up having all the ideas, then you are not encouraging your people to use their skills to the full. Your job is to develop your people, and that means getting them used to coming up with both new ideas and ways of implementing them. One of the most effective ways of doing this is to coach. As the saying goes: '*If we do what we always did, we will get what we always got.*' So in the ever-changing and complex world in which we live, innovation and creativity are at a premium – your job is to encourage it in others, not just come up with all the ideas yourself.

> The main aim of coaching is about better performance

Skills for effective coaching

There are a number of skills that the effective coach should be able to demonstrate and these include those shown in Figure 4.1.

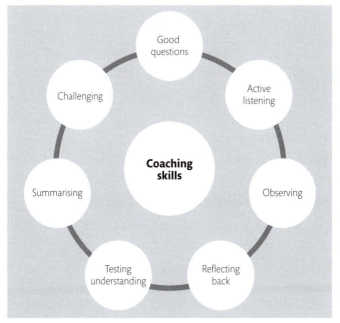

FIGURE 4.1 The skills required of an effective coach

Good questions

If I had an hour to solve a problem and my life
depended on the solution, I would spend the first
55 minutes determining the proper questions to ask,
for once I know the proper question, I could solve the
problem in less than 5 minutes.

Einstein

One of the key skills in coaching is to be able to ask effective questions. This isn't easy – we find that people tend to tell and give advice rather than think of the right question to ask. The humanist psychologist Carl Rogers tells us that our inability to communicate is a result of our failure to listen and respond effectively. So it is very important for a coach to set aside their natural tendency to give advice and to focus on asking good questions and listening to the answers.

So what is a good question? Many questions are not actually questions but merely displaced statements, or, worse still, accusations. We often make judgements and assumptions about what the other person is saying and this stops us from truly listening. We need to suspend these judgements and assumptions (this suspension is sometimes called bracketing). A good question is one that does not make assumptions or judgements, either in the way it is framed or in the tone in which it is asked.

> A good question is one that does not make assumptions or judgements

A good question is one that:

▌ makes the coachee truly reflect on the situation

▌ obliges a person to look at an issue from a different perspective

▌ allows enough time for the coachee to answer it

▌ does not betray or give the coach's own answer to the issue

▌ helps the coachee focus on solutions rather than on who to blame for the situation

▌ challenges people to question their own assumptions

▌ is open and helps the coachee truly think and reflect.

Questions should not be leading, in other words they should not be prejudiced towards a certain response. For example: *'We are in agreement on that, aren't we?'* You should try to limit the number of closed questions, which are those which can be answered with a yes or a no. For example: *'Do you agree? Do you support this? Do you like this?'*

Here are some examples of good coaching questions:

▌ What have you already tried?

▌ Imagine this problem has already been solved. What would you see, hear, feel?

▌ What's standing in the way of an ideal outcome?

▌ What's your own responsibility for what's been happening?

▌ What early signs are there that things might be getting better?

▌ Imagine you are at your most resourceful. What do you say to yourself about this issue?

▌ What are the options for action here? So, what's the next/ first step?

▌ How does that feel?

▌ Say more...?

▌ Can I check that I have really understood the points that you are making here? What you feel/think is...

▌ So, to summarise so far...

Active listening

This means that you are able to focus on exactly what the coachee says *and* how they say it. It means paying attention to the paralinguistics (the tone of voice, for example) and the body language. The well-known research by Professor Albert Meharabian tells us that when emotions are involved, words count for only 7 per cent of the meaning, with body language accounting for 55 per cent and paralinguistics for 38 per cent. Remember that Professor Meharabian tells us that this distribution holds true only when people are talking about emotional issues and not all of the time. His research has been criticised, but what all researchers do agree on is that paralinguistics and body language are critical aspects of all communication.

Observing

Your coachee will usually not be aware of their body language or paralinguistics, or even of the amount of times they say a particular word. An example of this is when Mike was teaching managers from a large national corporation how to coach. In one real coaching example, the coachee mentioned the word 'guilty' six times without being aware of it. It is then that the coach has to pick up on the word and explore what is behind it.

Often someone will lean forward and show much higher energy during the session when they talk about a particular person or subject, but they are not aware of doing so. It's your job as coach to point it out to them. Don't make assumptions about what it means, just point it out and then ask them what it might mean. For example, during a coaching session Simon is describing his work in a fairly bored way. He is leaning back in his chair and speaking in a flat, monotonous voice. Then he mentions a particular aspect of his job and a recent example of his work, and he suddenly moves forward, his eyes light up, his voice becomes stronger and more energetic.

Your task as a coach in this situation is to point out to Simon that at a particular point in the conversation he behaved differently. Then ask him why that might be. This usually leads to a much greater insight by the coachee.

Reflecting (behaviour identification)

Building on what we described above, the coach needs to notice the words, feelings, emotions and posture, and also needs to skilfully reflect them back to the coachee. The first step is noticing, but then it is necessary to reflect the behaviour back to the coachee and ask them what that might mean. In the example above we might say, *'Simon, I noticed that when you spoke about a particular aspect of your job, you sat up straighter, your face looked more animated, and your voice became very enthusiastic. Can you tell me about that?'* What we must not do is to fall into the trap of interpreting that and telling the coachee what it means.

> The coach needs to notice the words, feelings, emotions and posture

Testing understanding

You need to make sure you are fully clear about what the coachee means. It's very easy to misunderstand or, worse, make assumptions. So take a moment to test your understanding by saying something like, *'Can I just check that you meant X, for example'*, or *'I'm not quite clear what you meant by that.'*

Summarising

It is essential that you as the coach keep track of the conversation, so that you can summarise where the conversation has got to. So from time to time you might say something like, *'Cecile, let me summarise where I think we are.'* This gives Cecile an overview of the conversation and also enables her to either add more information or indeed correct any inaccuracies or misperceptions.

Challenging

One of the key jobs of the coach as we see it is to challenge the coachee's thinking and assumptions. But this needs to be done in a positive and elegant way. So you might just ask, *'Are you sure about this?'* or *'Can I just challenge your thinking here?'* or *'Are you making an assumption here?'*

How to coach

We have found two models particularly useful as practical frameworks for coaching. We don't recommend that you stick blindly to any one model, but they can be very useful when you are starting to use coaching in a more structured way.

One such model is the GROW model, developed by Sir John Whitmore, where the manager will use the structure to remember to find out the coachee's Goals, Realities, Options and Will. The idea is that the coach explores the coachee's specific goals and objectives, before then moving to exploring what is going on in reality, what has been happening, what people have done and said, who is involved and so on. Then the coach has the coachee develop a number of different options, before moving on to asking about the degree of will or commitment, and what energy the coachee has in order to take specific actions. It can appear a fairly obvious model, but it helps you to take a more structured coaching approach rather than just giving advice, so in practice it is very useful to have a model like this. In reality, many managers start to coach without having fully explored the specific goals and then find themselves stuck.

We have created a modified version of this structure and added a couple more Rs to the process (see Figure 4.2). The first extra R reminds us to specifically ask about Relationship as well as for facts and figures.

▌ What is the coachee feeling?

▌ What is the emotional reality?

▌ Who else is involved and how are they feeling?

There is a real danger that managers will be tempted to skip the emotional realities involved.

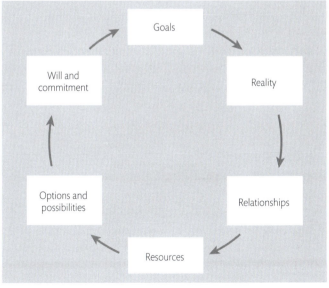

FIGURE 4.2 GRRROW model

Source: Mike Brent, adapted from Sir John Whitmore

The other R we add is for Resources, by which we mean, what are the strengths and resources that will help the coachee to move forward? When have they been successful in addressing similar issues, for example? What are the resources and competences that will help them resolve the issue? You cannot focus simply on what the coachee cannot do.

Managers are often tempted to skip over the coachee's goal and go directly to reality questions. Typically, managers are very good at asking analytical questions concerning reality, but not so good at asking about the emotional and psychological realities. As for options, the trap here is for the manager to give *their* options and opinions rather than ask the coachee for theirs. Many people also forget to ask about will and commitment, assuming that it will just somehow happen. It is important to ask specific questions about the degree of will and commitment and to get specific actions and dates and to follow up on these.

The second model we find useful is the OSKAR model, developed by Solution Focus experts Mark McKergow and Paul Z. Jackson. OSKAR stands for Outcome, Scaling,

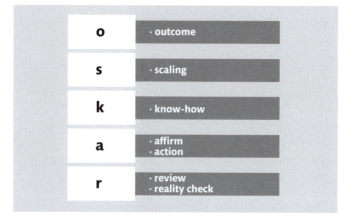

FIGURE 4.3 The OSKAR model

Source: Used with permission, McKergow and Jackson, 2007

Know-how, Affirm and action, and Review and reality check (see Figure 4.3).

> It is important to ask specific questions about the degree of will and commitment

Outcome

The coach starts off by finding out the coachee's desired outcome. This is possibly an even better question than simply asking for goals. Many of us don't have a specific idea of what our goals are in a particular situation, but being asked about the outcome forces us to reflect on what we would like to achieve. This in itself would be a good coaching session even if we didn't get any further. The coachee would then have a much clearer idea of what they wanted.

Scaling

This means finding out where the person is in relation to the desired outcome on a scale of 1 to 10. So, for example, if my outcome is to have a better relationship with my boss, then the question would be, '*Where on a scale of 1 to 10, with 10 being high and 1 low, would you say your relationship is right now?*' If the coachee answered that it is a 3 out of 10, for example, the next question would be, '*Where on the scale would you like it to be?*' To which the answer might be a 5. From this you would be able to ask, '*What would a 5 look like or feel like?*' You could then ask specific questions about what your boss would be doing, or what you would be doing in a 5 out of 10 relationship.

This forces you to imagine positive specific actions that you and your boss would be taking in this improved relationship. It also has the advantage of making you realise that you are not just a passive victim but have an active role in this situation. It's not just about what your boss could be doing differently but also about what you could do differently. Once you are able to imagine what your boss could be doing differently, this allows you to ask your boss for specific behaviours that they can then respond to.

Know-how

This is about finding out what the coachee's strengths are. What resources do they have? When have they overcome a similar type of issue? Too often people see themselves as passive victims with no resources, but in fact it is very likely that they have strengths and resources that could be brought to bear on their current issue. Again the coach will help the coachee to focus on their resources and energy rather than their weaknesses.

Affirm and action

This is a two-step process. First, the coach will give a positive affirmation to the coachee. This is based on ideas around positive psychology, which we discuss further in Chapter 14. The coach will reflect back something positive that the coachee is already doing in the situation. This is important because it gives self-belief and confidence, but also, and importantly, it gives energy. It might be something like, *'I like the way you stood up for yourself in that difficult situation. It showed real strength and resilience.'*

It's not easy for most managers to give positive affirmations, but we feel it is critical to notice people's positive behaviours and strengths and above all to share them with the coachee. Again, we go into more detail in Chapter 14.

The second step of the process for Affirm and action is to ask the coachee in some detail about what specific actions they will now take to address the issue – the more specific the better. Don't allow generalisations, make sure you get specific actions with time frames. If the coachee says, *'I'll talk to my manager,'* that's not good enough. Ask them not only where and when but more importantly *what* exactly they will say and *how* they will say it. Get them to say it out loud to you so that you get a sense of how it might come across.

Again, you might meet with some resistance here, but if you don't press for specifics then you are not helping the coachee to really think the issue through.

As a matter of principle it is better to get the coachee to take a series of small steps rather than going for ambitious targets which they are unlikely to achieve. For example, if you were coaching someone who does no physical activity, you might want to hear them say they will start by taking a 15-minute walk every day rather than them tell you they will go from nothing to running five miles a day within a week.

Review and reality check

This can be done in two separate stages. First of all during the coaching session, when you can look back and summarise what has been said, and then agree on specific actions and time frames. It's the time to ensure that you are both in agreement with what has been said and agree a time to meet up and review the actions. The second step is the review meeting after the coachee has had a chance to implement their agreed actions. This is where you compare what the coachee said they would do with what they actually did and what happened as a result. This may lead to more coaching or a tweak in agreed actions, plus any other follow-up plans. Think of it as a sort of reality check: what did they actually do and do they need to come back to Outcome and reconsider what they want to achieve and what is actually possible?

Traps to avoid when coaching

When you are coaching someone, it is very easy to develop unhelpful behaviours and bad practices. Here are some of the traps you may fall into:

▌ *Taking the monkey.* There is an expression, 'to take the monkey', meaning that you end up taking on other people's problems and issues. This is extremely common in management for two reasons. One, the manager very often thinks that their job is to solve problems, and the other is that, as a result of hierarchy and command and control culture, many employees have become used to letting someone else do their thinking for them. So as a coach you must avoid taking responsibility for other people's issues. Your job is to make them do the thinking, not solve the problem for them.

▌ *Giving advice.* In our workshops we observe many examples of managers whose default style is to go immediately to giving advice – what we call the '*Why don't you?'* or '*If I were you'* style of coaching. We know that's it's difficult to resist giving advice, and of course sometimes advice is necessary, but it is not coaching! So instead of giving advice, put it aside and tell yourself that you are there to help the coachee find their own answers and use the coaching processes mentioned to focus your mind on getting the coachee to reflect and come up with options.

▌ *Offering a solution.* An employee comes to the manager with an issue and instead of asking questions and listening, the manager feels obliged to offer their solution to the employee. Apart from the fact that the boss is not always right, this leads to a mental laziness on the part of the employee, who is not being forced to think the issue through and come up with different courses of action.

▌ *Interrupting.* It is such a common thing for managers to do. Sometimes it comes from arrogance, but often it comes from a sense of trying to be helpful. But interrupting people is an insidious thing. People have a basic psychological need to be heard and listened to, and you are denying that if you interrupt them. You are also telling them that their point of view is less important than yours, which is disruptive to the coaching process.

▌ *Not being fully present.* Be fully present and in the moment when you are coaching. It means that the most important thing you can do is give the coachee your presence and full attention. It's not always necessary to know what your next question is in advance, but if you are fully focused on the coachee, with your mind firmly in the present, you will notice more and hear more and your next question will be easier.

▌ *Inappropriate non-verbal behaviour.* Your coachee will be observing you at the same time as you are observing them. This means that you have to pay attention to your non-verbal behaviour. You need to be able to show interest and energy. Avoid showing any impatience, don't fidget and don't look at your watch during the session, it will just make the coachee feel that they need to hurry up. Remember to set guidelines about confidentiality and timing at the start of the session.

▌ *Being distracted.* This can easily happen. You, too, have many things on your mind and you can allow your thoughts to wander during the process. This means that you are not focusing on the present situation, not listening closely enough to what is being said and not paying attention to the nuances and changes of tone. You then stay on a superficial level and don't pick up on the underlying issues. Also, your coachee will notice that you are not paying attention and will conclude that you are not taking them or the issue – or both – seriously.

▌*Interrogating*. This can be a risk if the coach starts asking too many closed questions in an impatient and hurried way. The coachee does not feel listened to and gets the impression that the coach is not trying to explore the issue together but is simply looking for facts which could be used to criticise. You must also pay attention to tone of voice. The process can seem like an interrogation if you are not taking account of the coachee's feelings and emotions.

▌*Blaming and judging*. If you become critical of the coachee and their actions, and they feel that you are blaming them, it will make them defensive. The sense that you are being judgemental comes from the words you use, of course, but also from the tone of your voice. When coaching someone you must remain open-minded, neutral and non-judgemental. You are trying to get at the reality and truth of things, and criticising is the surest way of making the coachee clam up, so you will have achieved nothing.

When should we coach?

The short answer here is, 'all the time'. As mentioned above, one of the objections to coaching is that it takes too much time. The opposite is true: simply telling people what to do is what actually consumes time! Too often we are tempted to use the 'Why don't you' model, instead of asking people what their thoughts and options are. Almost any interaction can be done in a coaching style, although we don't recommend asking people for their different options and alternatives in the middle of a crisis. However, coaching is an opportunity to review past crises and learn from them.

Take advantage of everyday situations to do some immediate coaching by asking your colleague what they might do, rather than simply giving your opinion or advice. We call this 'in the moment' coaching. There are countless opportunities to do this in your regular interactions with people. There are also planned coaching sessions where you have the opportunity to sit down with your team and discuss issues of concern to them. But what do you do when you see an opportunity to coach someone but they don't come and ask you for some coaching? As well as the 'in the moment' coaching style described above, we can recommend a methodology to help in this situation.

If you see an area where you think someone could have improved their performance, first of all ask them how they think they did. If they take a moment to reflect and answer that they did well but that they could still do even better, then you have an opportunity to coach them. If, however, they say they did it perfectly, then you can ask another, more specific question about their performance. If this time they acknowledge that they could do better, then you have an opportunity to coach. If they do not see any potential for improvement (but you do), this time it may be worth pointing out some factual information. An example would be, '*I noticed that you interrupted the client on several occasions.*' They then have the option to admit to a potential improvement in their performance, thus giving you a coaching opportunity.

If once again they deny that there is any need for improvement, then at this stage you will have to point out that in your opinion they need to improve and that you would be happy to coach them. By this time you have given them every opportunity to analyse their performance and recognise the development they need. If they are not able to do this, you may have to have a serious conversation about their attitude.

In recent years coaching has become very popular, with many senior executives enjoying long-term coaching relationships. This is a significant move from how coaching used to be regarded as remedial and for poor performers only. Nothing could be further from the truth: coaching is about developing potential and performance and we can all benefit from it. After all, the top performers in sport and the arts all benefit from coaching – why would we be any different?

Many managers will point out that the culture of coaching people does not work in their country, often saying that people of a specific nationality do not understand or value the coaching approach. We have run coaching workshops for managers all over Europe, as well as in Thailand, China, the US, Mexico and Switzerland, with participants from India, Pakistan, Japan, China, Thailand, Singapore, Taiwan, Korea, Hong Kong, Puerto Rica, Mexico, the US, UAE, Qatar, Indonesia and Malaysia.

In general our experience suggests that most managers accept that a coaching style of management is beneficial, even if they sometimes have difficulty in actually implementing the style. However, there is a sizeable number of practising managers in all cultures who really do not see the need to adopt a coaching style. Cultural theory would tend to suggest that we would see more resistance in the Far East, Middle East and South America, but our experience has not borne this out. There are, however, some influencing factors in managers' attitudes to coaching, and culture is certainly one of these.

If we take an example from one culture where we have had some experience – China – we see that the hierarchical system and the respect shown to one's superiors is sometimes a barrier to effective coaching. One example of this is Sarah Qing Tian, an HR manager for General Electric in Beijing, who tells the following story about implementing coaching in China in her previous organisation.

CASE STUDY

Even for those managers who tried hard to coach their staff, it finally seemed to become 'telling' and 'instructing'. Why? There were two main reasons. One involved the employee's perspective and the other the manager's perspective. In China, if an employee comes to their manager, they expect an answer from their manager, not a question like, *'How would you do it?'* The employee's reaction to a question like that would be, *'If I knew, I would not ask you.'* Another scenario might be, *'The manager obviously doesn't know the solution, that's why he/she is asking me!'* and the manager might risk losing face and not appearing to be experienced and knowledgeable.

As Sarah points out: 'Chinese people are not so likely to openly point out mistakes made by their boss during a coaching session. The Chinese education system is based on learning by heart, and listening to the orders of the teachers. Thus, it is naturally expected for a manager to give clear direction, and detailed orders. A manager who is managing by asking questions might risk losing respect among their employees and subordinates, and their actions being misunderstood by them.'

Although we have taken an example from China, it is worthwhile pointing out that we have seen examples of effective coaching by Chinese managers and examples of poor coaching in the UK, Europe and the US. So there are some cultural barriers to implementing a coaching style, but in reality it depends on how skilful the coach is. We have seen that telling or instructing can work when we are dealing with simple puzzles, where there is a clear answer, but it is useless when dealing with more complex problems or dilemmas, no matter what the culture.

> There are some cultural barriers to implementing a coaching style

In a culture where coaching is not common, it is still possible for the skilled manager to highlight that we are dealing with a complex situation. In this type of case there are no simple answers, only different options. As such they are first of all interested in finding out more about the situation, the person or persons involved, what they have already tried and what they and others are feeling. At the very least they are getting the employee to think and to reflect and become part of the solution instead of depending on the manager to tell them what to do.

Tips for success

▌ Don't over question. Questions might, and on occasions should, challenge, but it's not an interrogation.

▌ Ask the coachee to summarise often.

▌ Be aware of your preference for giving advice and the coachee's request for advice.

▌ Resist giving advice too quickly – use advice sparingly.

▌ Try to reframe and offer different perspectives through questioning.

▌ Identify restraints, especially internal ones.

▌ Balance your reality questions with questions that move the issue on. In other words, don't try to get all the facts.

▌ Remember to use the naïve question – this can be enlightening and powerful.

▌ Tune into, understand and read emotions as well as logic.

▌ Use 'what if' questions.

▌ Ask how important the issue really is – this can sometimes be quite revealing and you can use the scaling technique we mentioned earlier.

▌ Build on what the coachee is actually saying rather than inventing new questions.

▌ Coaching should always lead to actions.

▌ Challenging is a key aspect of coaching, but do it constructively.

▌ Pay attention to the coachee's non-verbal communication as well as their words.

Influencing

Influencing is the essence of leadership.

Professor Gary Yukl, University of Albany, New York

In this chapter we propose to share the basic principles of influencing. For a more complete discussion of this interesting and essential topic, please refer to the book we have written in the same series, *The Leader's Guide to Influence* (Pearson, 2010).

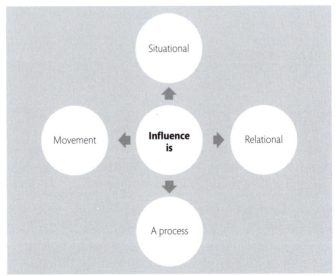

FIGURE 5.1 The four key aspects of influence

What do we mean by influence? We believe that there are
four key aspects of influence, as shown in Figure 5.1.

Influence is situational

Every situation is different and you will need to adapt your
influence style and approaches depending on the context.
You probably have a preferred way of influencing others, but
it may not be the right one for every situation. So you need
to become aware of your preferred influencing approach
and work out whether you need to flex it for these different
situations. This involves analysing each situation before you
start to influence and working out the best approach for that
situation.

This is more difficult than it sounds. We have found that
most managers have a default influencing approach. They
use it regularly and it has proved successful in the past,
so they use it again and again. But that's no guarantee that
it will work in the future. You have to move out of your
comfort zone and learn to use different approaches.

Influence is relational

Influencing happens between people, so again you need
to be aware of your own influencing approaches and the
approach others may favour. The onus is on you to read and
understand the other person and then influence in a way
that makes sense to them. Influencing is not based solely on
what you want to achieve, but also on understanding what is
meaningful to the person you are trying to influence.

A couple of tools are useful here. One is to create a
stakeholder map (see *The Leader's Guide to Influence* for a
fuller explanation) of your influencing issue and try to work
out what's in it for the person you are influencing. Let's face
it – if you have no formal authority and there's nothing in

it for the other person, you are highly unlikely to influence them. This means that you have to see each situation from the other person's perspective and then work out how to frame your influencing argument in that way rather than from your own perspective. We like to call this the SWIIFT principle – **S**o **W**hat's **I**n **I**t **F**or **T**hem?

> You have to see each situation from the other person's perspective

Another tool we have found extremely useful in relational influencing is something called the Spectrum model, which is a model developed by the late George Prince and Vincent Nolan. It involves building on other people's ideas rather than just criticising them. Typically in meetings, when someone proposes an idea we hear a lot of negative reactions, such as *'This will never work'* or *'We've already tried this'*. Or when people are trying to be a bit more positive about the idea they might say, *'I agree with your idea, Fiona, but…'* And then they proceed to disagree with it.

What Prince and Nolan suggest is that instead of either completely agreeing or disagreeing with an idea, you should actively look at what might be of value within the idea. After all, it's unlikely that in a meeting where complex issues are being discussed one single person will have all the answers. You look for anything of value within an idea, so you focus not on what you disagree with or dislike but on what you see as useful. That might be as high as 90 per cent or as low as 10 per cent, but of course you don't mention specific numbers. What you can say is something like, *'What I like about your idea, Fiona, is…'* or *'I like your focus on…'* and slot in the aspect of the idea that you find of value. Then the next word you use is not *but*. Instead you would add *and*, so your phrase would be, for example, *'I like your focus on using external suppliers for this contract, AND we could try using a new one on this occasion.'* So, in effect what you are doing is noticing something good in the other person's idea, appreciating it and then linking and building on their idea by adding your own thoughts.

But what happens if you think that the other person's idea has no value at all? In that case we would still want you to express an appreciation, perhaps along the lines of, *'I like your enthusiasm. It shows you are motivated by the issue.'* Then, instead of being judgemental or critical, you can either voice your concern,*' I'm slightly worried about...'* or ask an open question. So your sentence might look like this: *'I like your enthusiasm, Mike, it shows you are really motivated. How exactly do you see it working in practice?'* What you are doing here is suspending any critical judgement and yet still forcing the other person to confront the specific realities. They are then likely to focus on the question and admit that there are still some shortcomings to their idea. This is far more engaging and productive than you simply telling them their idea is rubbish!

By the way, this can be an extremely good way of dealing with the Extroverts in your team, who often have a tendency to think out loud without necessarily having explored all the implications of their idea.

Influence is a process

Influence is about building and developing your reputation and credibility in the various situations you face. Most of the time you will be influencing people you see on a regular basis, whether clients, bosses or colleagues, so you have to view it as an ongoing process and not as a one-off event. You will be influencing in a specific context – at home or at work, for example – and therefore need to take their context into account.

Seeing influence as a process and not as an event has a few implications. Because you will see the people you are influencing on a regular basis, it means that you cannot afford to mislead them. If you do, your reputation and credibility will suffer and your influencing ability will suffer. On a more positive note, it gives you the opportunity to influence in stages. In many cases you will not be able to convince someone immediately, so viewing influencing as a process gives you the chance to progress in small steps – and build agreement over time. Imagine it as climbing a staircase step by step. Your aim is to get right to the top, of course, but since influencing is a process, you might not be able to get to the top in one go. You might need to aim for the halfway step in your first meeting, then gradually move up the rest of the staircase.

> Viewing influencing as a process gives you the chance to progress in small steps

Let's take the example of trying to convince your boss to give you a pay rise. You could go in and ask for a rise and expect him or her to say yes right there and then. You'd probably be disappointed! Or you could view the objective of getting a rise as a process. You might then work out what the different steps in that process were. Step 1 might be to do some research into pay grades internally and externally. Step 2 might be getting to know your boss better and finding out what he or she values in their people. Step 3 might be to analyse your work and results and see which activities are the most productive. And so on – viewing influence as a process will help you to plan and prepare and thus be more effective.

Another advantage is that it enables you to build agreement along the way. If you are in a meeting, make sure you get everyone's agreement on a specific point before you move on to the next one. Not just nods, but ask everyone specifically whether they are in agreement – and get them to say it out loud. That way even if you don't get to a full agreement on the original goal, you will at least have made progress and when you meet again you don't have to start all over again at the foot of the stairs but rather halfway up, since you will have ensured clear commitment on what has been agreed so far.

Influence is about movement

By that we mean it's not about winning or losing or even being right, but about getting the other person to shift their position, even if it is only a slight movement. In fact, the origin of the word influence comes from the Latin word '*influere*', meaning to flow into. The ancients believed that there was a mysterious force in the universe which 'flowed' into the earth and influenced it in different ways, for example by creating tides. If there is a shift or a movement in the direction you propose, then you can say that you have effectively influenced the other person even if they don't fully agree with you. So the lesson is to be realistic and don't expect to win every argument. Influencing is not about winning, it's a two-way process.

The following principles, used effectively, will help you to get that movement.

The ten key principles of influencing

Figure 5.2 shows ten key principles that will help you to become more influential. They are drawn both from our own work with managers and from research by experts such as Dr Robert Cialdini and Jay Conger.

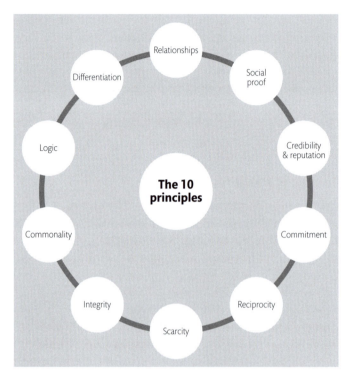

FIGURE 5.2 Ten key principles for gaining influence

1 Relationships

For us, the very first principle to use when you are trying to influence without authority is to build effective relationships. This means using common courtesy, being polite, friendly and sociable. It means being interested in the other person and expressing that interest. Specifically it involves effective listening, asking good, open questions, linking to others' thoughts, and building on them. So it involves the use of 'and' rather than 'but', as we described above. Other ways of building effective relationships include:

▌ having a good sense of humour

▌ making sure that you notice positive behaviours in other people

▌ giving praise and compliments

▌ noticing people's non-verbal language

▌ adapting your body language and voice to theirs

▌ listening to the kind of language they use and reflecting it back to them.

Psychology tells us that we like people like ourselves, so try to empathise and build rapport by showing curiosity and interest in the other person.

2 Social proof

Another strong influencing principle is social proof. That means that if someone you like, respect or admire is influenced by something or someone, there's a strong chance that you will be influenced by that person also. For example, Mike was hesitating about buying an iPad, as he was unsure of its usefulness and worried that it was just a gadget. But when his respected business school colleagues Steve, Narendra and Fiona bought one, that social proof was enough to convince Mike to get one. The basis of this principle is that we tend to be more readily influenced about an issue when we see others we hold in high regard have already bought into the idea.

Many organisations use this principle. The online book retailer Amazon uses it extensively. If you are a regular user you will notice that when you order a book, the site will immediately give you a list of similar books that others have bought, in the hope that you, too, will buy them. It also indicates how many books have been sold and gives a star rating based on customer reviews. This principle suggests that we are far more likely to buy a product if many others, or others who are similar to us, have bought it.

3 Credibility and reputation

We need to have a certain credibility and reputation if we are to be believed, and if we don't have formal authority in a specific situation, it needs to be replaced with our natural authority. There have been multiple experiments about the power of authority and even though we tend to respect formal authority less nowadays, we are still inclined to believe experts.

> We need to have a certain credibility and reputation if we are to be believed

Dr Ben Goldacre, in his book *Bad Science*, mentions the extraordinary power of the placebo effect. This effect can be amplified using the authority principle. In a controlled experiment, patients with abnormal symptoms but no specific medical diagnosis were split into two groups. One group was told that the doctor wasn't certain what the matter was. The second group, meanwhile, was given an authoritative diagnosis in a confident, straightforward way. After two weeks only 39 per cent of the first group were better but 64 per cent of the second group got better.

This is also linked to credibility – to be an effective influencer you need to establish your credibility. Imagine for a moment a situation where you had very little credibility and no formal authority. How could you possibly be influential in that situation? So the question you need to answer is: in each influencing situation, where do you get your credibility from? How can you increase your credibility?

We are lucky enough to work in a beautiful building originally built in the 1200s and then rebuilt in 1808. It's an imposing building with an interesting history – Queen Elizabeth I lived there for a time. We have an excellent reputation and are highly ranked in various publications. The building, its history and these rankings enhance our credibility as teachers. But how do we establish our credibility if we are teaching in the Middle East or in China, or the US where our participants have never heard of Ashridge? We then need to look at other sources of credibility – our qualifications, our books or our expertise and experience, for example.

A word of warning, though: authority can be contrived or manipulated, so make sure your credibility is real.

4 Commitment

There are two sides to commitment: one is getting other people to commit and the other is clearly demonstrating your level of commitment. Let's talk about other people's commitment first. People are generally inclined to respect their own commitments, especially if these are validated in public. So as an influencer you need to make sure people clearly state their commitments in public. When you make a statement in a meeting, don't just assume people will agree or throw out a general 'We're all agreed, right?' statement. Get people to clearly and specifically state their agreement publicly. If they are unsure, see that as an opportunity to convince them. It's much better in any case that they voice their disagreement now where you can deal with it rather than pretend to agree now and then sabotage things behind your back later.

Another thing is to start small. Many people try to convince others to commit to fairly large objectives, but it is much better to start small and get clear commitments, before going for a larger objective. It's preferable to chunk your objectives down to bite-size pieces – and get commitment on one step at a time.

When you are demonstrating commitment it's unlikely that it will be hugely influential if you are showing lukewarm interest in the idea or process. You need to demonstrate passion, belief and knowledge if you are to be convincing. This can be very difficult for leaders when they are not actually personally committed to a decision but they still have to implement it. So what can you do in this case? First, you need to remember that as a leader you may not always be completely convinced about a course of action. Of course, you should take the opportunity to attempt to influence that course of action, but once the course of action has been decided, it is your responsibility to ensure that it happens. If you disagree with the decision, then you have a choice. Either tell yourself that you can live with it and will have opportunities to influence the implementation process, or, if you really can't live with it, it may be time to change jobs. What you must not do is to moan and gripe about and publicly disagree with the decision. This will affect your credibility and reputation as well as your relationship with your bosses.

> You need to demonstrate passion, belief and knowledge if you are to be convincing

Remember, as a manager it's highly unlikely that you will agree with every decision taken within the organisation. So even if you do disagree, make sure you are as positive as you can be when communicating and implementing the decision. You don't have to lie – you can share that while you are not fully convinced about the decision, you are fully committed to the organisation so you will give 100 per cent to implementing it.

5 Reciprocity

Psychologist Michael Tomasello tells us that humans are
an extremely social species, so we have a clear need to
collaborate as well as to compete. What that means is that if
you do something for someone else, they are inclined to feel
a psychological need to do something in return.

Here is an example from the world of charitable organisations.

CASE STUDY

A while ago the Red Cross sent Mike several lovely cards
and included a few rather attractively designed cardboard
bookmarks. The value of these cards and bookmarks
probably added up to no more than a few pence, as the Red
Cross themselves admit.

But because the cards were attractive Mike decided to use
them, and sent them to friends. At the same time as the
Red Cross sent the cards they also asked for a donation.
Now Mike of course meant to send a donation but didn't
quite get round to it, so was feeling some slight pressure
to reciprocate by sending a donation. The Red Cross then
sent some more cards – and again they were attractively
designed and as Mike never quite gets round to buying
Christmas cards, he used the cards. And again he didn't
quite get round to sending a donation! So now he felt even
more psychological pressure to send in a donation. Then
he realised that this was a great example of the principle of
reciprocity. So Mike decided to use this in his lectures as an
example of reciprocity. Then, having used the cards and used
the example in his work, he felt so much pressure to donate
that he made a donation of five times what he was asked for.

So the question here is, what can you give to others? Rather
than waiting for people to do things for you, look at some of
the things you could be doing for others. The principle could

be: get your reciprocation in first! If you do look to give first you will find that it creates a subtle change in people's behaviour. But watch out: don't just do things for others in the expectation that they will immediately do something for you. It's a lot more subtle than that.

6 Scarcity

This principle is perhaps not the easiest one to use in everyday influencing situations, but it is clearly a strong principle used in marketing in order to influence people. Most adverts tell us to buy now before (the always limited) stocks run out – for example, when discounts are limited in time.

The UK airline British Airways, like many airlines, uses this principle in its online ticket purchasing. When you look at a flight, the website now gives you information about how many seats are left – for example, it will tell you that there are only two left at this price! Does it make a difference? You bet. One estimate says it is worth around £50 million to BA annually.

Another way of looking at this principle is to try to differentiate yourself from others and thus be a more scarce resource. For example, if you have a particular skill, how can you leverage that? In which particular area might that skill be needed? So how can you use this principle? How might you show that you are a scarce resource?

> If you have a particular skill, how can you leverage that?

7 Integrity

This is about trust. Put simply, if you are trying to influence someone and don't have formal authority over them, you need them to trust you. If they don't, and therefore don't believe what you're saying, you have absolutely no chance of influencing. Our research at Ashridge shows us that most people trust their immediate boss (83 per cent) and the leader of the organisation (69.8 per cent), but that still leaves 17 per cent of people who reply that they do not trust their immediate boss and 30.2 per cent don't trust the top leader in their organisation. So, how do you create trust?

Here is a list of things that our research has shown to be useful in creating and maintaining good levels of trust:

▌ Be fair and consistent.

▌ Be open to being challenged.

▌ Listen to and involve people on a regular basis.

▌ Agree on common goals and focus for your team.

▌ Clarify yours and others' expectations.

▌ Delegate, give people some autonomy and discretion in the way they do things, don't micro-manage.

▌ Give the reasons behind decisions and not just the decisions.

▌ Make sure you do what you say you will do – in other words, don't talk the walk, walk the talk!

▌ Create an atmosphere of mutual respect.

▌ Have plans and processes in place for potentially difficult issues that may arise.

▌ State clearly the organisation's principles and core values – and respect them.

So next time you are about to influence someone, ask yourself how much you think they trust you perhaps on a scale of 1 to 10. If it's not a 7 or above, it's unlikely you will be successful.

8 Commonality

To use this principle effectively you need to forget about trying to strongly advocate your position. Rather, it is about enquiring into what the other person is thinking and feeling and then looking for common ground between the positions. If there is no common ground at all, it is highly unlikely that you would be able to influence without authority. Your only recourse then is to try harder and find some potential common ground or find someone else who does have authority and use them to influence the person.

Let us give you an example. Sue is trying to influence her colleague, John. So Sue thinks a lot about her proposition and the logic of her argument. She states her proposition by saying something like, *'We ought to recruit a new salesperson.'* If John is not in favour of Sue's idea, he is likely to express that by saying something like, *'I disagree.'* Whereupon Sue immediately replies by coming up with her rehearsed position. She will focus on the rightness or logic or validity of her arguments and will come up with all sorts of reasons why John should agree. But what does Sue know about John's position? So far she knows only that he disagrees, nothing more.

So the idea here is to have Sue enquire into John's position rather than simply advocating all her good reasons. As Sue enquires into John's position, what she is effectively doing is expanding his position and thus increasing the likelihood of finding some commonalities or common ground between the two positions. Once these have been established she can make links between the positions and increase her chances of influencing effectively.

The key skill here is asking questions rather than simply expounding ideas. By doing this, Sue will also create an emotional link between herself and John. This is important because inclusion is a fundamental interpersonal need. We will look more closely at how to ask effective questions in Chapter 14. Becoming effective in this area will also build on our very first principle: building effective relationships.

> The key skill here is asking questions rather than simply expounding ideas

9 Logic

Logic is necessary but not sufficient. Of course, a clearly illogical argument doesn't make for good influencing. But you need to make the numbers and logic talk, and tell a story. It is important to ensure that logic and numbers are backed up by clear and easy-to-read visuals and graphics, in order to support and give examples of what the numbers mean. Some writers are brilliant at this – the American writer Bill Bryson is particularly good at it.

Logic alone will not convince, however. Let's look at the example of smoking. Many doctors still smoke cigarettes. Why? If we, the general public, know that smoking causes 95 per cent of lung cancers, then surely they do too. But the figures alone are clearly not enough to convince people to stop smoking. According to Dr Ben Goldacre, in *Bad Science*, doctors who actually worked with patients suffering from lung cancer stopped smoking more than others. They could see at first hand the devastating effects, whereas the numbers on their own are not as influential.

We once met a manager who told us that his influencing problem was that he was always right but his team didn't get it – in other words, they didn't think he was right at all.

We gently pointed out to him that while being right was certainly an advantage, it wasn't actually enough and that he would need to think about people's emotions, his impact and their perspectives on the issue. Yet he remained convinced that being right was enough – even though it clearly didn't work in his case. Being right is fine, but it's rarely enough to convince.

We believe emotion is necessary and logic is never enough. People are not influenced by logic alone. Being right is an advantage, of course, but it is not enough. Many people prefer to use a purely logical approach and then fail to understand the necessity of the emotional connection, and therefore they fail to influence effectively.

10 Differentiation

One of the main ways to influence others when you have no formal authority is to make sure you have established some differentiation between your position and others. If your argument is the same as everybody else's, you won't be terribly influential. If your business proposition doesn't distinguish itself from the competition, you won't be very successful. One way to create differentiation is to tell a story. A story contextualises information and gives it meaning. It adds emotion and therefore has a greater impact. Cognitive psychologist Roger Schank tells that humans are not ideally set up to understand logic but they are set up to understand stories. So think about how you can present information as a story or narrative.

Tips for success

▌ Be patient – influencing is a process, not an event.

▌ Flex your style to suit the situation.

▌ Identify what's in it for the people you are trying to influence.

▌ Remember, influencing is a two-way process – this involves compromise.

▌ Analyse the situation to ensure you select the most appropriate strategies and techniques.

6
Facilitating

What we call leadership consists mainly of knowing how to follow. The wise leader stays in the background and facilitates other people's process.

John Heider, US management author (b. 1960)

What do we mean by 'facilitator'? The origin of the word comes from the Latin *facilis*, which literally means to make things easy. So if you facilitate a meeting or a process you are there to make it as easy and as useful as possible, in other words to get the best out of the people at the meeting.

You know what it's like when you have a meeting and no one is there to keep things under control, to keep things progressing and not getting stuck. You have those who have nothing to say but take a long time to say it and those who have a lot to say but who may lack confidence and say very little or nothing. Then you might have extraverts who think as they speak and introverts who are thinking but not speaking. You have others who bring up new topics that have nothing to do with the current issue but who talk at great length about something that is meaningful only to themselves and adds nothing to the meeting. So, someone has to facilitate this process or watch the meeting descend into chaos. Yet often we don't think to appoint a facilitator, or if we do, we ask someone to take notes or write on the flip chart, or perhaps act as chairperson – but there is no discussion about what the role is and what the person should be doing in that role.

The role of the facilitator

There are three major areas to focus on when facilitating:

▍ the work the group are doing, in other words the task, the WHAT

▍ the process of accomplishing this task, the HOW

▍ the relationships and dynamics inside the group, the WHO.

Often groups will tend to focus on the WHAT, to the exclusion of the HOW. The WHAT is tangible and real and results oriented, while the HOW is often intangible and ambiguous, and is therefore not addressed at all in meetings. The WHO is fairly obvious but is frequently not done very well. The facilitation of the group therefore involves addressing all: the WHAT, the HOW and the WHO.

Facilitating is about making sure that everyone who wants to be involved is involved. So your task might be to bring in some people who look as if they want to participate but are not getting the opportunity. Or it might mean stopping others who are hogging the limelight. Or yet again, keeping the meeting on track when it starts meandering away from the subject. Or it could involve giving people back a sense of control.

The following are some of the key aspects of the facilitator role:

▍ Create the environment in which people can feel free to give ideas, discuss them frankly and challenge each other.

It helps to make sure that everyone can get involved in the meeting.

▌ Ensure that there is structure and process to the meeting so people will agree on the timing of the meeting, the structure and the ground rules. These should be created by the group itself, and might include aspects such as no interruptions, no personal attacks and no distractions.

▌ Pay attention to what is said, how it is said and, perhaps more importantly, what is not said. What might be the elephant in the room?

▌ Intervene as and when necessary to keep things progressing. The intervention might be to bring someone in, to shut someone up, to challenge an assumption, to summarise what has been said or to notice a pattern that others are not seeing.

▌ Check that the meeting is actually making progress and not getting stuck on one subject or going round in circles.

▌ Notice what's below the surface during the meeting and bring it to people's attention. Be the person who dares to point out the elephant in the room.

▌ Summarise at the end of the meeting and ensure that everyone is in agreement with that summary.

▌ Conclude the session and check on what agreement and actions have been reached and gain commitment to these actions from each person involved. Hear from everyone, albeit briefly, to ensure that they have understood.

> Create the environment in which people can feel free to give ideas

Useful tools and methodologies for the facilitator

There are a number of tools that it could be helpful to be aware of as a facilitator. We cannot go into depth in this chapter, but we would like to give an overview of those we believe to be most useful:

▐ the Spectrum model

▐ intervention styles

▐ Neuro Linguistic Programming (NLP)

▐ advocacy and enquiry.

The Spectrum model

This methodology, which we mentioned in Chapter 5, is based not on criticising or judging other people's positions but on focusing exclusively on the positives and then building on these. So, for example, if Marco shares an idea with the team and the others think it's not a good idea, then instead of just dismissing the idea, which is often what happens, what they actually do is to focus instead on something they do agree with, or find useful or valuable. So they would say something like: *'Marco, what we like about your idea is its focus on communicating to all the team.'* Now clearly they didn't like all of the idea, and instead of saying something like 'We agree but...' and then criticising his idea, they can now build on his idea by adding something like, *'...and we could also ensure that we ask them to give us specific details about the numbers of sales visits they make.'* This makes for much more effective meetings, more creativity, more options and more involvement.

Intervention styles

This is another useful model when acting as a facilitator. We have adapted it from original work done by John Heron, author, academic and expert in facilitation. In this model (see Figure 6.1) there are six styles that the facilitator can use to intervene in any process.

The top three in the figure are what we might call authoritative interventions, that is to say Prescribing, Informing and Challenging. The bottom three are facilitative interventions: Releasing, Discovering and Supporting.

Authoritative interventions

▌ Prescribing is telling someone what to do, much like a doctor would prescribe a medicine. They would tell you exactly what to take, how to take it and when to take it.

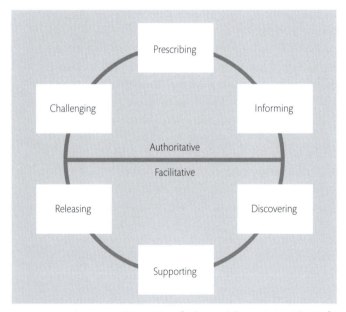

FIGURE 6.1 Intervention styles (adapted from John Heron)

▌ Informing is giving information to someone without any judgement. For example, you can find information about human resource management from the CIPD website (**www.cipd.co.uk**).

▌ Challenging is when the facilitator wants to raise someone's awareness about an issue or behaviour of which they are perhaps unaware. For instance, you might say, '*You say that you value listening but you have interrupted Susanna twice.*'

Facilitative interventions

▌ Releasing is allowing someone to open up and express emotions rather than denying or suppressing them. This might take the form of a question like, '*How does this make you feel?*' or simply allowing the emotion to be expressed.

▌ Discovering is where you encourage people to think for themselves rather than giving them the answer. For instance, using open questions such as '*How might you approach that?*'

▌ Supporting is encouraging people and affirming their qualities so you would recognise and praise something that is done well.

The idea here is for the facilitator to be able to use all of these styles in a skilful and appropriate way. We often make the mistake of using too much of the authoritative styles, and therefore not using the facilitative ones enough, or vice versa. Another trap is just to use one or two styles, to the exclusion of the others. The skilled facilitator will know when and how to use all of these styles. They will know, for instance, when to challenge, when to support and when to move from one style to the other.

> The skilled facilitator will know when and how to use all of these styles

Neuro Linguistic Programming (NLP)

It might be helpful for a facilitator to be aware of how language can often be abused and distorted, and NLP has many good examples of how this happens and how to deal with it when it does. One common abuse is the misuse of universal quantifiers. These are words such as *always, never* and *all.* Here is an example of the common misuse of the word 'always'. Juanita says, *'Andrew's always picking on me!'* In reality, Andrew is not always picking on Juanita. He may have disagreed with her a few times, but there is a big difference between a few and always. And it also means she is ignoring the many times where Andrew has actually agreed with her and supported her.

You can challenge this by asking Juanita: *'Is he really always picking on you? Has there ever been a conversation where Andrew has perhaps agreed with you?'*

The skilled facilitator can, and should, pick up and challenge these abuses of *always* or *never* or *all*, which are extremely common in exchanges, meetings and when dealing with conflict. It also happens when people use their experience of one person in a category and then apply it to everyone in that category. A common one we hear is, *'Engineers don't understand emotion at work.'* The way to challenge that is to say something like, *'All engineers don't understand emotions? You mean there isn't one engineer in the world that understands emotions?'* Clearly the phrase 'engineers don't understand emotions' is absurd and untrue, but generalisations like this happen all the time, and when you are facilitating dialogues, conversations and meetings, you need to intervene and challenge this type of language.

Advocacy and enquiry

In any conversation or meeting there needs to be a balance between advocacy and enquiry. Advocacy is when people tell you what they are thinking, give their point of view and support a particular course of action. Enquiry is when people ask questions, explore the other person's thinking and refrain from giving their own ideas. Clearly, any meeting where there was pure advocacy without any enquiry would be a disaster. Equally, if no one puts forward any ideas, suggestions or opinions in the meeting and everyone just asked questions, it would be a farce. Usually in the meeting as a whole there is a reasonable balance, but it can happen that one person takes only one perspective and advocates only their position, without either asking any questions or giving any reasons for their point of view. This is unbalanced and also unskilled, so again you as a facilitator need to pick up on this and intervene to help the person perhaps ask questions and listen to the others, or encourage them to share the thinking behind their perspective and not just their conclusions.

Strategies for facilitator intervention

The facilitator must intervene skilfully and in a calm way. This suggests being totally in control of your emotions, being balanced, and ensuring that your body language and tone of voice are under control. It's generally good to have some evidence before you intervene. For example, if you think someone used an inappropriate word during an exchange, you should be specific and feed that word back to the person.

The facilitator must intervene skilfully and in a calm way

So it might go something like this: *'Harold, you used the word "idiot" when arguing with John a moment ago.'* Or: *'Steve, you interrupted Rachel when she was speaking about the need to put in proper HR procedures.'*

Sometimes you rely on your gut feeling and you can give feedback to someone on their tone of voice or facial expression. So you can say something like, *'Rebecca, you sounded angry when you talked about Diana.'* It takes a lot of skill, energy and courage to be able to do this. But the objective is to help the group or team work more effectively together and thus achieve better results.

One of the issues the facilitator has to face is resistance and confrontation from others. Here are some tips about what to do when you are faced with resistance and confrontation:

▌ Accept the reality.

▌ Don't resist.

▌ Listen.

▌ Ask open questions and explore the other person's point of view, without advocating your position.

▌ Don't judge or criticise their view. This just leads to defensiveness.

▌ Try to look at their perspective from different angles. Look for anything positive.

▌ Look for any points of agreement (see Spectrum model).

▌ Find the purpose of the resistance or confrontation. In other words, what is motivating it? It might have nothing to do with the facts and everything to do with emotions.

We believe that every people manager must be able to be an effective facilitator. You will need to use these skills to manage meetings and in project groups, and on an individual and interpersonal level throughout your career.

It's about relating to people effectively and helping people get the best for themselves and their teams.

Tips for success

▌ Be present by focusing on what is happening now – don't dwell on the past or think too much about the future.

▌ Focus your attention and concentration on each speaker.

▌ Notice and observe people's reactions, emotions and non-verbal communication and body language.

▌ Have the courage to step in and intervene when necessary.

▌ Know when to step in and when to stay back.

▌ Listen carefully to what is being said – and how it is said.

▌ Respect other people's points of view and perspectives on the topic.

▌ Create empathy and rapport with the team members.

▌ Develop a sense of trust and being trusted by the team.

▌ Have an overview of the meeting.

▌ Build on and link to people's ideas during meetings.

▌ Step in before any conflict has gone too far, but don't block it completely (See Chapter 10 for more on conflict).

Team building

Talent wins games, but teamwork and intelligence win championships.

Michael Jordan

Introduction

In our companies and organisations we all have to work in teams in order to get things done. Most things actually get done in teams. Our research at Ashridge shows that 69 per cent of managers work with five or more teams and that 88 per cent are responsible for at least one team's performance.

Karen Ward, Mary Kennedy and Mike Brent identified five factors of complexity for teams:

▌ the need for solutions to multi-faceted ambiguous dilemmas

▌ the need for a multidisciplinary approach in tackling these

▌ the need for diversity of viewpoints

▌ the need to work across and outside organisational boundaries

▌ the need to work in dispersed mode across geographical and time zones, in other words so-called 'virtual' teamwork.

The research also identified that working and getting the best from a team wasn't an easy thing to do. It found that:

▌ the failure rate of complex teams is as high as 50 per cent

▌ only 12 per cent felt that their organisation had effective techniques to evaluate team performance

▌ 98 per cent wanted a balance between task and process yet felt their organisation wanted the task achieved at any price.

> It's not finance or strategy or technology that is the ultimate competitive advantage but team working

Patrick Lencioni, in his book *Overcoming the Five Dysfunctions of a Team*, states that it's not finance or strategy or technology that is the ultimate competitive advantage but team working, because it is so powerful and yet so rare. Our experience supports the fact that real teamwork is actually quite rare. In this chapter we will give you some ideas in order to help you work more effectively in teams. We will look at the what, why and when of teams, a range of team processes and team dynamics, but before we do that let's look at what makes a good team. You might like to examine this list and reflect about the teams you lead or are a member of, and assess whether or not these features apply:

▌ a clear motivating goal

▌ a strong sense of commitment

▌ the ability to work interdependently

▌ team members who are competent and who have complementary skills

▌ effective ground rules and standards of behaviour

▌ good interpersonal communication and relationships

▌ an appropriate style of leadership, depending on the type of team

▌ internal support and recognition for each team member

▌ external support for the team and recognition for its work.

The what, why and when of teams

Why do we need teams? The world, as we know, is a complex place. The US military has coined the term 'a VUCA world', which stands for Volatile, Uncertain, Complex and Ambiguous. In this VUCA world, it's highly unlikely that one person alone can deal with the complexity of the situations we face. We therefore need a number of people working together towards the same goals, but with diverse opinions on how to get there.

What is a team? The usual definition of a team is 'a small group of people with complementary skills and a common purpose'. Small, because too many people and it is ineffective. The accepted range for an effective team tends to be between 5 and 12 people, although Wharton Business School Professor Jennifer Mueller concludes that 6 is optimal. But although significant, the number of people is not as important as the quality of the people and the type of leadership demonstrated within the team. Teams need complementary skills because you need people with different skills and preferences to gain the maximum amount of diversity and common purpose. For the team to achieve anything it needs to have discussed and agreed its common purpose. It's actually quite amazing how many so-called teams there are which have not discussed the issue of complementarity or indeed common purpose.

Researchers Jon Katzenbach and Douglas Smith made the useful distinction between working groups and teams. They are not the same thing and have different goals and objectives, need different skills and produce different results. Working groups, for example, share information, perspectives and insights. They place their focus on individual goals and accountabilities, and not on taking responsibility for results other than their own, whereas teams also focus on mutual accountability and responsibility. There are a number of other differences between working groups and teams. Teams, for example, also have a specific team purpose as well as the more general organisation mission to follow. A group is likely to have a specific leader whereas a real team is able to share leadership roles.

The main thing to remember is that just because you call a group of people working together a team, that doesn't magically make them a team. Until you work to develop specific team attributes, it will be a working group. That said, effective working groups can be more productive than ineffective teams. But at their best, real teams will outperform working groups.

At their best, real teams will outperform working groups

As we have mentioned, the world we are living in is an extremely complex one, a VUCA world, so it is increasingly difficult for one person (no matter how brilliant and how high up the hierarchy) to have the answer to all the problems and dilemmas our organisations face. However, we do still sometimes face less complex issues, ones which are fairly well known and where there is no uncertainty. These issues can be described as 'puzzles', and they can be solved by individuals, so when faced by puzzles we can often act and decide alone. When we face more complexity and less certainty about an issue, we can describe it either as a problem, which does have solutions, or as a dilemma that actually doesn't have any one single solution. When

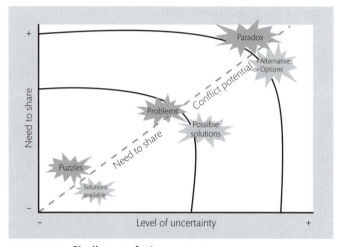

FIGURE 7.1 Challenges facing a team
Source: Critchley, B., and Casey, D. (1984). 'Second thoughts on team building.' *Management Education and Development*, Vol.15, Pt.2, pp163–75

faced with a problem we need to work in teams in order to leverage diversity, get different opinions and challenges, and see how we can use the collective intelligence of the team to find the best possible solution. When faced with even greater uncertainty – a dilemma, we still need to use a team, but now we need a high-performing, complex team to help work out the different options and possibilities for action. So we must expect divergence and challenge and truth at this level, which demands a highly effective team (see Figure 7.1).

Team processes and dynamics

For teams to be as effective as possible, the team leader needs to focus on not only the task but also the processes that support the team's way of working and the dynamics between the team members. These are essential areas but are often overlooked. They include the following areas:

Engaging people in teams

The team leader has a clear role in helping the team to be effective. Researchers (Robinson and Hayday) at the Institute of Employment Studies looked at what it takes to be an engaging manager. They were trying to find out what kind of managerial behaviours were considered to be effective in engaging the team and leading to better performance. In general the study revealed that praise and positive feedback when the team did well, plus encouraging ideas and suggestions from the team, led to improved team performance.

The behaviours that led to team leaders being seen as engaging were:

▌ communicates and makes clear what is expected

▌ listens to, values and involves people

▌ is supportive

▌ is target focused

▌ shows empathy.

Interestingly, four out of the five are relational and interpersonal skills. The study also asked people what managerial behaviours led to disengagement.

The answers were:

▌ lacks empathy and interest in people

▌ fails to listen and communicate

▌ being self-centred

▌ doesn't motivate or inspire

▌ is aggressive.

So as we can see, engaging with the team is important because effective engagement leads to better performance.

This leads us now to discuss how the team can be managed or led.

Team leader or team manager?

The quick response to this question is that a team needs to be both managed and led. Managed, because certain things need to happen to certain people at certain places and at certain times. Processes need to be in place, details looked at, delays respected, etc. But a team that is only managed and has no leadership will not be able to address the complex dilemmas that we face nowadays. They will only be able to do more of the same – manage existing issues rather than create innovative options to help resolve these complex dilemmas. In short, if the team is managed but not led, you will probably see evidence of planning and organisation and control. Team leadership needs to address issues such as ensuring that the team has motivation and energy and inspiration. It needs to look at how effectively the members work together so that the team is really more than the sum of its parts.

Another key point to make is that the leader should have as a primary objective to enable the team to lead itself. That is to say that every team member should ultimately be able to assume leadership within the team. In an interview with the *Guardian* newspaper on 16 March 2013, English rugby player Tom Croft says: '*A year ago the coaches were guiding players through everything. Now you go into leadership meetings and it's completely player driven.*' That is where you need your team to get to, and it's your responsibility as the team leader to develop the people in the team to the level where they can begin to lead as well.

> The leader should have as a primary
> objective to enable the team to
> lead itself

Working effectively together

Here are some key tips for working well together that we
think are essential:

- Listen – and we mean listen properly – to each other.

- Show respect for each other.

- Enquire into what the others are saying – an effective team
  needs to expand its thinking before coming to conclusions.

- Diverge before you converge as a team. In other words,
  allow challenge.

- Don't criticise but build on each other's thinking.

- Take responsibility – don't blame others.

- Have genuine positive intent towards the other team
  members.

- Have clear rules and processes.

The stages of team development

Probably one of the best known models of stages of
team development is Bruce Tuckman's model, which he
developed when working with the US Navy. The model,
shown in Figure 7.2, follows the stages of Forming,
Storming, Norming and Performing (to which he later added
Adjourning).

FIGURE 7.2 Tuckman's stages of team development

Source: Tuckman, 1965

Let's look at each of these stages.

▌Forming

This is when the group first forms, and as you might expect it is characterised by hesitation in terms of how to approach both the task and the people. People will look for clear direction and may rush into a task focus without looking properly at processes – how they want to work together. Roles and responsibilities are not clear at this stage. In this stage the leader's role is to reassure, explore people's motivations and preferences, and help team members get to know each other. It will be important to launch a conversation about the team's common purpose.

▌Storming

The next stage is one characterised by conflict and jostling for position. Power becomes an issue, who has it and who doesn't. Cliques may form, leading to some people belonging and others not. Emotions can run high.

The team leader's job here is to leverage any conflict. That means using any conflict in a constructive manner. There is a danger here that conflict might be completely avoided and thus close down opinions. The team leader needs to ensure any differences of opinion are not personal and facilitate any conflict so that it is positive. It is important to remind the team of their common purpose. Clearly, if this purpose has not been established it will make things very difficult.

> **Power becomes an issue, who has it and who doesn't**

Norming

Here we see a more cohesive group. There is a clarification of roles and responsibilities and goals become clearer and harmony becomes important. So conflict and disagreement may be discouraged at this stage. Hopefully at this stage we begin to see discussions about team processes and how people will work together as well as a focus on the task. Delegation within the group often happens here. One of the team leader's tasks here is to create sub-groups to ensure an effective working approach. It is at this stage that tasks can be delegated, once you have found out team members' preferences and skills. Ensure that any disagreement can surface and make sure that the group doesn't fall into the trap of groupthink.

Performing

At this stage the group is working well together, is tolerant of diversity, has a strategic awareness and has developed a common vision. Members have more flexibility and autonomy and actively help and support each other. The team leader will want to keep the team at this stage for as long as possible. There may be new members, so they will need to be properly integrated into the team. Achievements should be recognised and celebrated. Promote and encourage diversity and make the case for it. Keep the big picture in mind and remind the team constantly of their purpose.

Adjourning

This is when the team breaks up, which is a natural part of any team's life cycle. It can be the end of the whole team or just some members leaving the team. The leader's role at this stage is to focus on two things: learning and appreciation. Anybody who is leaving the team should be properly thanked and recognised for their contributions – this is extremely important and often overlooked. Then it's useful to go over what the team contributed to the organisation and what the team members learned, and how that learning can be fed back to the organisation. This is so that future teams can benefit and not reinvent the wheel. Then the team should celebrate together. This will help them move on as there may well be a feeling of personal loss as the team breaks up. It also means that team members will go into any new teams with a positive sense of energy.

This model is useful as it raises awareness that teams do go through different stages. It means that you can pay attention to the stage of the team and then try to intervene to move it on. It can also be helpful to realise that it's normal for teams to go through a period of being wary, then having conflict, then developing rules and ways of behaving, and then achieving results. But there is a danger in thinking that this is a straightforward, linear process. Have you, as a team leader or team member, been part of a team that moved skilfully and seamlessly through these stages? Of course not! In reality, it's much, much messier than that. So it may be more helpful to view the model as a dynamic process which sees the team forming, then going through storming, norming and performing and adjourning as a circular, ongoing process (see Figure 7.3). Then of course it would have to go through a reforming process when any new member arrived.

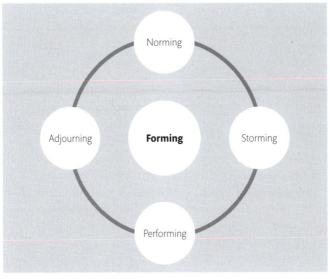

FIGURE 7.3 Stages of team development
Source: Adapted from Tuckman, 1965

Complementary teams

Effective teams need to be complementary, that is, they need
to have people with different preferences, approaches and
thinking. Otherwise the team will all end up thinking in the
same way and being unable to create diverse and innovative
options. We have worked with teams that were complementary
and those that consisted of people with similar preferences
and outlooks. In our view, a team that consists of people with
the same way of working and similar viewpoints will have
limited effectiveness, and may not even deserve to be called a
team – it is more likely that they are a group.

> The potential disadvantages of the
> complementary team relate to time
> and conflict

The potential disadvantages of the complementary team relate to time and conflict. A lot of time will be spent in discussion and if conflict arises, which is inevitable when there is difference, and if that conflict is not well handled, it can be a waste of time and lead to loss of energy and focus.

Perhaps the best known research into complementary teams has been carried out by Meredith Belbin and then later by Charles Margerison and Dick McCann. The research showed that certain types of work had to happen within the team for it to be effective and, building on that, that team members had certain preferences as to which type of work they carried out. If the team members' preferences covered the spectrum of work that needed to be carried out, you could say that it was a complementary team. The researchers created different models and also questionnaires that enable teams to examine and reflect on their complementarity, or lack of it. We have worked extensively with both of these questionnaires and found them to be extremely useful as a way for teams to examine the idea of complementarity, but also as a catalyst for team dynamics – how the team could work together.

Margerison and McCann's research found that the different types of work that had to be addressed by the team were as follows:

▌ Advising – gathering and reporting information.

▌ Innovating – creating and experimenting with ideas.

▌ Promoting – exploring and presenting opportunities.

▌ Developing – assessing and testing the applicability of new approaches.

▌ Organising – establishing and implementing ways of making things work.

▌ Producing – concluding and delivering outputs.

▌ Inspecting – controlling and auditing the working of systems.

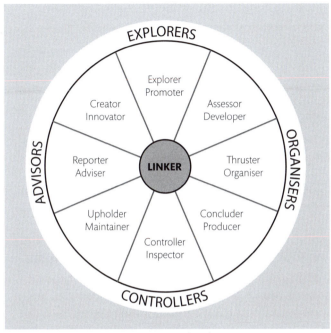

FIGURE 7.4 Team management wheel
Source: Reproduced with permission from TMS Development International Ltd, 2013 www.tmsdi.com

▌ Maintaining – upholding and safeguarding standards and processes.

▌ Linking – coordinating and integrating the work of others.

From that they examined the roles that people preferred and found eight, with the added need for someone to link and facilitate the different preferences (see Figure 7.4).

The eight team management roles

Each of these roles brings a different range of skills and perspectives to the team.

▌ *Reporter-Adviser* – someone who is supportive, tolerant and a helper. A collector of information, knowledgeable and flexible but who dislikes being rushed.

▌ *Creator-Innovator* – someone who is creative, imaginative and future oriented. This person enjoys complexity and often likes research work.

▌ *Explorer-Promoter* – someone who can sell and persuade and who likes varied, exciting, stimulating work. They are influential and outgoing but may be easily bored.

▌ *Assessor-Developer* – someone who is objective and analytical. An experimenter and developer of ideas who enjoys prototype or project work.

▌ *Thruster-Organiser* – someone who prefers to organise and implement things, who likes to set up systems. Quick to make decisions and results oriented.

▌ *Concluder-Producer* – someone who is practical and values effectiveness and efficiency. Often production oriented and likes schedules and plans. Takes pride in producing goods and services.

▌ *Controller-Inspector* – someone who is strong on control and is detail oriented. An inspector of standards and procedures. Often has a low need for people contact.

▌ *Upholder-Maintainer* – someone who is conservative, loyal and supportive. Personal values are important to them and they often have a strong sense of right and wrong.

Ideally, the team will have members who collectively have preferences about all these areas, or at least, members who have enough flexibility to have some degree of preference. If the team is indeed a complementary one, then there may be issues to address, such as potential conflict and different perspectives. This is where the team leader has to demonstrate their linking and facilitation skills (see Chapter 6).

If the team is not a complementary one, the team leader can assume the role of the missing preference area, ask one of the team members to assume the perspective of that role, or invite other people with these preferences to join the team on either a permanent or a temporary basis.

Further information about these instruments can be obtained from Belbin Associates (for the Belbin team roles) at **www.Belbin.com** and TMS Development International Ltd (for the Margerison–McCann Team Management Profile) at **www.tmsdi.com**).

Why teams go wrong

We have worked with hundreds of teams in Europe and worldwide and have seen that while many teams are very effective, just as many seem to get it wrong. There are many reasons for this and they tend to fall into three categories: bad habits, not surfacing issues and not fully exploring the fact that team leadership is more like a dilemma than a puzzle.

Bad habits

Bad habits include:

▌ being too individualistic

▌ unskilful conflict management

▌ laziness

▌ having too much of an internal focus

▌ dismissing other people's ideas

▌ being closed to external people and new members (acting like a clique).

In order to avoid the above, let us suggest some good habits:

▌ Support each other in the team.

- Build on each other's ideas rather than criticising or dismissing them.
- Focus on goals rather than on scoring points.
- Focus on results, not personalities.
- Be open to new members and ideas.

Clearly, this is not an exhaustive list – feel free to add your own good habits to it.

> Many processes that the team needs to be aware of are under the surface

Not surfacing issues

Many processes that the team needs to be aware of are under the surface. It's like an iceberg where 90 per cent of the ice is below the surface. These are issues such as:

- How should we work together?
- How much do we trust each other?
- How do we challenge each other?
- How do we really feel about each other?

But in order for a team to be truly effective these issues must come up to the surface, so the team leader must focus on:

- surfacing issues and discussing the 'undiscussables' that are creating barriers (the elephant) in the room
- leveraging conflict – not suppressing it too quickly but making the best use of the dynamic interchange of ideas
- generating ideas – not blocking
- reflecting on implications and learning as well as acting
- building and linking people's ideas rather than simply criticising them

▌ openly addressing the dilemmas that all teams face.

The latter is such an important aspect of team leadership that we will explore some of these dilemmas below.

Dilemmas facing teams and the team leader

Our Ashridge colleagues, George Binney, Gerhard Wilke and Colin Williams, researched a number of team leaders over a four-year period and found that they faced some interesting dilemmas, or as they put it, zones of choice. Leaders had to decide, for example, between time spent managing upwards versus time spent being there for the team. Clearly, both are necessary, and perhaps you as a team leader have a preference for and ability in one of these choices. So if you enjoy being there for the team, what happens about managing your boss's expectations? Interestingly, the leaders felt that it was an either/or choice, but in reality these are what our colleagues called 'zones of opportunity', where the leader can move around in these zones and adapt to the needs of the moment, rather than being stuck on one end of the zone of opportunity.

Among other choices that you as a team leader may expect to confront are the following:

▌ *Understanding – enquiring while knowing.* This is about the balance between the team leader knowing what to do, what course of action to take, and finding out more information, asking open questions and making sure they get more thoughts and feelings from the team members, before taking action.

▌ *Direction – acknowledging limits while imagining a better future.* This is about realism and pragmatism versus vision and imagination. On the one hand, the leader needs to acknowledge reality and constraints, but on the other hand they need to be able to give the team some kind of hope and vision.

▌ *Timing – waiting and seeing while accelerating progress.*
This is about when to make decisions. Does the leader
surge ahead with decisions based on limited knowledge or
wait until things are clearer when it might be too late?

▌ *Relationships – getting close while maintaining distance.*
This is about how the leader relates to their team – how
close do they get? Do they get close and personal with the
team so that they develop a good working relationship?
Or do they stand back, remain impersonal but have some
distance and perspective? Too close and there are dangers,
but too far away and there are different dangers. What is
the right degree of closeness?

▌ *Loyalties – putting your own needs first while serving your
organisation.* This is about who you put first, your own
needs or those of the organisation. Put your own needs
first all the time and you risk being seen as selfish. Put the
organisation's needs first all the time and you risk ruining
your health and personal relationships. Where are the
boundaries between these needs? If you haven't reflected
on some boundaries, it will be difficult for you to know
when and how to balance these conflicting needs.

▌ *Authority – letting go while keeping control.* This is
about how much you empower your people versus how
much you keep control and authority. Give away all your
control and you risk being seen as an ineffective leader,
give away none and you are seen as a control freak who
micro-manages and doesn't trust their people.

▌ *Self-belief – showing vulnerability while being strong.* This
is about the need to be strong and confident, which the
team will need at times, versus the need to demonstrate
that you are not perfect and that you don't know
everything. If you are too confident then people won't dare
to try things for themselves. If you are strong enough to
reveal vulnerabilities, people may find it easier to connect

with you and then share their doubts and vulnerabilities with you.

You might like to ask yourself the following questions about the teams you operate in. Which of these zones of choice are you facing in your role as a team leader? What are your default preferences? Which end of the spectrum comes easiest to you? What are the implications of these preferences? How might these be holding you back? How can you expand your choices and try to incorporate both ends of the spectrum of these zones of choice? How can you experiment and be flexible?

Remember, building an effective team takes time and effort and is a continuous process. It won't happen just by chance. One team expert we spoke to is former English and British Lions rugby player Nigel Melville. Nigel has impeccable team credentials, having played in and coached rugby teams at the highest level. He is currently President and Chief Executive of the US Rugby Federation. Nigel tells us that teams in business and organisations are becoming more and more like teams in sport. Performance is constantly being analysed, deliverables checked, and people constantly reviewed and assessed.

> Building an effective team takes time and effort and is a continuous process

As the pace of business increases and the environment becomes more complex, teams are being held even more accountable. The implications are that you need to keep reinventing both yourself and your team and that you can evolve constantly. It also means that like sportsmen and sportswomen, the team will have to reflect on how they manage their energy, fitness and health.

Tips for success

▌ Constantly discuss and remind team members of the team's purpose.

▌ Involve the team in setting up a clear list of what is acceptable and what is not acceptable behaviour.

▌ Focus on mutual interest rather than self-interest.

▌ Drive out fear! If there is fear, you won't get honesty in the team. And if you don't get honesty, you won't get reality.

▌ Ensure that everyone is involved in the team and avoid narrow cliques which exclude those who are not in the clique.

▌ Leverage conflict rather than avoiding it. Make sure that your team knows how to disagree and challenge positively and constructively.

▌ Agree ways of working together. This is often overlooked in the rush to accomplish the task.

▌ Pick up on nuances of behaviour, and what is not said. Be aware of people's non-verbal communication.

▌ Recognise and respect any differences in culture and look for ways to leverage that diversity.

▌ Don't assume that a group is always a team.

▌ Don't underestimate intangibles, emotion, mood and feelings.

▌ Don't always be the first to speak up or take the lead. Let others take the lead and use your confidence to support them.

▌ Don't jump to the first idea. Be creative – look for different options and possibilities.

Motivation

8

*Motivation is the art of getting people to do what you
want them to do because they want to do it.*

Dwight D. Eisenhower

Motivation has been a major management issue for
decades and has been the subject of many research
studies by such eminent people as Abraham
Maslow, Frederick Herzberg, Douglas Macgregor, Clayton
Alderfer and John Hunt. Much of what they found remains
applicable today. However, in recent years there have been
significant changes to working practices, including:

▌ more attention to work life–balance

▌ flexible working practices

▌ virtual working

▌ home workers

▌ a focus on performance objectives.

In this chapter we'd like to consider motivation from both
the individual and organisational perspective – first, what
motivates and engages you, and second, what you can do
to contribute to other people's motivation and engagement
at work.

Motivation and the individual

Understanding your own motivators and being clear in your mind about what it is that satisfies and engages you at work, and what it is that dissatisfies you, is key. As a starting point you might like to examine the list in Table 8.1 and indicate those areas that you regard as key to your motivation and those areas that are less important.

TABLE 8.1 Motivation factors

Factors that motivate me at work	Level of importance			
	Very important	Fairly important	Not very important	Completely unimportant
A high basic salary				
Performance-related pay/incentive schemes				
Clear career advancement within the organisation				
Challenging/interesting work				
Job security				
Formal recognition for success within the organisation				
Opportunity to use your creative abilities				
Having the authority and freedom to run your own show				

Factors that motivate me at work	Level of importance			
	Very important	Fairly important	Not very important	Completely unimportant
Opportunity to continually learn and develop my skills and knowledge				
Working in an innovative environment				
Working for an inspiring manager				
Allowing individual decisions to have an impact on the organisation				
Being treated with respect				
Doing work that is of value to society				
Working for an organisation that takes social and environmental issues seriously				
Working for a leading organisation				
Working in a pleasant environment				
Regular feedback on performance				
Working with like-minded people				
Others – please add own motivators below:				

Source: Adapted from the Ashridge Management Index 2012

Once you have identified what it is that motivates you, it is important to share this with your boss and others so that they understand how to create the environment to enable you to work at your best.

The Ashridge Management Index 2012 identified 19 key factors for motivation and engagement. As well as listing all the items in Table 8.1 and asking people to think about the level of importance to their motivation, we asked them to assess the same list in relation to what their organisation relies on for motivation and engagement.

Table 8.2 shows in the second column the seven factors identified by individuals as their main motivators in order of importance. The third column indicates those factors that they believe the organisation relies on.

TABLE 8.2 Motivators and the organisation

Individual importance	Motivators	Organisational use
1	Challenging and interesting work	2
2	Opportunity to learn continuously and develop skills and knowledge	5
3	A high basic salary	6
4	Having the authority to 'run my own show'	15
5	Clear career advancement within the organisation	8
6	Knowing my decisions have an impact on the organisation	14
7	Performance-related pay and incentive schemes	1

From these results it appears that employees believe that their organisations are significantly off track in relation to the motivation and engagement of their people. Individuals appear to be motivated more by opportunity and interest in what they are doing, with the extrinsic rewards being of less importance. However, organisations appear to rely on performance-related pay and incentive schemes as a major element of their motivation and engagement strategy.

> Individuals appear to be motivated more by opportunity and interest in what they are doing

This does not mean that individuals are not at all interested in the external motivators. What it does mean is that organisations are missing a trick in that pay, reward and other incentives are often of less importance than more internally driven behaviours such as doing something because it gives them pleasure, it develops a skill or it is the right thing to do.

Understanding what motivates you is vital for your happiness and contentment at work. It will also help you to make the right choices about jobs, organisations to work for and careers to explore.

CASE STUDY

Murray is a 28-year-old IT specialist. Since finishing university he had worked with a small niche consultancy as the IT specialist. This role gave him a lot of opportunity to develop his IT and business skills as well as giving him freedom to work from home and manage his own time and workload.

After five years Murray felt he wanted to try something new, so he began to explore possibilities. He was fairly clear about his needs. In particular he wanted to work in a team environment with others who were similarly skilled where he would be challenged and would develop his IT skills. He was offered several jobs with well-known organisations, all of which were well paid and had great conditions of service – he turned down all of these jobs because they did not match his particular skill set and current aspirations.

In the end he joined a small start-up because it 'felt right, it was an exciting opportunity and the young MD was inspirational and visionary'. This wasn't the most lucrative job but in his view it would be the most stimulating and developmental. His choice was not just about reward but about challenge, interest and opportunity to grow and develop.

Motivation and others

Once you understand your motivators you can then think about how you can help others within your organisation to be motivated. As most people are more engaged by intrinsic motivators, it is important for you as a manager to be willing to spend time getting to know others and to understand their particular needs. This takes time and energy. The process of getting to know others, i.e. communicating with them, will in itself act as part of the motivational process. Authentic communication is a big part of motivation and engagement. Interacting with others to explore their needs and wants from a job will show that you are interested in them and your subsequent actions will back this up.

We believe there are five key factors in a person's working life that are important to consider for motivational success. Figure 8.1 shows how these five factors interact and have an impact upon your own and others' motivation within an organisation.

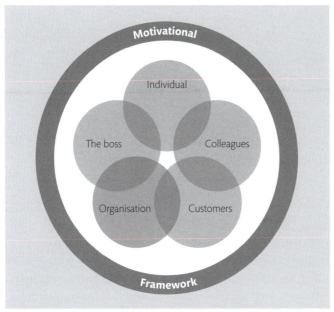

FIGURE 8.1 Five factors for motivational success

The organisation

This provides the structures and processes, including reward systems, performance management processes, training and development and interesting work. Having the systems alone is not enough, of course – the organisational culture will affect how all of these processes are applied in practice. So there needs to be:

▌ a clear vision

▌ effective communication processes

▌ appropriate consultation practices

▌ quality decision making

▌ a culture of mutual respect and trust.

These are lofty principles and it is the responsibility of each and every person in the organisation to aspire to them. Having top-level support and commitment is beneficial, but each of us can adhere to a set of principles that makes us motivated in ourselves and also to help others be motivated.

> Each of us can adhere to a set of principles that makes us motivated in ourselves

The individual

You must be clear what motivates you and how you can satisfy these needs at work, and be willing to share this with others. Each one of us must take responsibility for our own engagement and motivation. The organisation can provide you with opportunities, but largely it is down to the individual to take advantage of them.

The boss

The boss plays a vital role. Bosses can make you feel appreciated, respected and valued by spending time with you to understand your needs and drivers. Once they know this they can play a crucial role in helping you to capitalise on and take advantage of opportunities that will enable you to work in a motivated and engaging environment. The boss should be one of the primary sources of feedback about your performance and given that feedback is regarded as one of the factors that help to keep people motivated, it would signal that as a boss you should develop your skill in this area.

Colleagues

Working with like-minded colleagues can be energising and motivational. To find these colleagues you need to share your values, needs and desires so that when working with others you can recognise how to get the best out of each other.

Customers (and clients)

Getting feedback from external stakeholders will help with your motivation. Knowing what external stakeholders expect of you and satisfying their needs is wonderfully motivating and rewarding. As a leader, when that feedback is given, ensure that you communicate to the people concerned. In fact, you should be actively on the lookout for positive external feedback.

> You should be actively on the lookout for positive external feedback.

Motivating high performers

We were interested in the question of whether a manager could possibly further motivate someone who was already highly intrinsically motivated. Could an external person actually play a role in motivation or does the motivation have to be completely personal? This led us to speculate about how performance is motivated in different areas, including the arts and sport, as well as in business. So we chose to speak to someone who understands both business and sport at the highest level.

Greg Searle is a management consultant and partner of the successful Lane 4 Organisation, originally created by sports psychologists and top sports performers. He is also unique in that as a sportsman he won three Olympic medals over a twenty-year period. According to Greg, the manager (or coach) can have a substantial role to play in motivation. Although athletes already have huge amounts of intrinsic motivation, it can and will fluctuate, given the massive demands placed on the athlete and their family. The manager can amplify existing motivation and sustain it over the long term. According to

Greg: 'You need high amounts of motivation just to show up, but you need even more to keep going.'

The same is true of people who come to work day in and day out. How can we sustain their motivation? Some of the ways the coach can do this are as follows:

▌ *Give focus within the focus.* The athlete is already highly focused, but the coach can point out specific details on which the athlete can focus even more. For example, if Greg was working out on a rowing machine, a fairly monotonous session, the coach could break the session into sub-goals and give him feedback on times, scores and data, thus making the session more interesting, rewarding and useful. Managers could usefully think about breaking down some of their team's less interesting tasks and agreeing on sub-goals, and make the link to how the achievement of the sub-goal leads to better overall performance.

▌ *Explain the importance of each and every training session.* Managers can do this, too. They can explain the importance of what appears to be a routine task, within the overall context and purpose.

▌ *Share the hard data.* Motivation is not just about the soft stuff, it's important to know the differences between performances. So even if the athlete feels they have done well, the coach can point out the hard facts. Similarly, a manager can point out the specifics of their performance to the employee and coach them when any issues are identified.

▌ *Show interest.* This is crucial, Greg believes. The coach, just by being there, and by being present, paying attention and showing the athlete that they are paying attention, can be a massive boost to motivation. Similarly, the effective people manager can help with motivation or perhaps, even more importantly, prevent demotivation by being present and paying attention to their team. This also means recognising the person's efforts and good work and offering positive feedback.

▌ *Link the athlete's hard work to achieving their dream.* In other words, the coach is supporting the athlete's dream while sharing their own dream with the athlete. Managers could learn a lot from this, by ensuring that they find out what their employee's dream actually is and then linking the person's work to the achievement of that dream. This is much more motivational than just sharing their own or the organisation's dream or vision.

It is also worth mentioning those areas that demotivate people. Common demotivators are:

▌ poor leadership, where senior managers are lacking in skill and capability

▌ poor or slow decision making

▌ not being valued

▌ poor, little or even no performance feedback

▌ micro-management

▌ organisational tolerance of poor performance

▌ people who whinge and moan all the time

▌ too many meetings

▌ hot desking

▌ poor communication

▌ no development or career possibilities.

Give some thought to what it is that demotivates you and pay attention to those people you work with to become aware of their demotivators.

A successful motivator will have a management style that encourages growth, development and experimentation. They will treat their people with respect and demonstrate trust in their ability to do their job. They also foster an appreciative organisational culture that promotes policies and processes to recognise good work and celebrate success.

Tips for success

As an individual:

▌ Have a clear sense of what motivates you.

▌ Actively look for work that fits with your personal motivators. For instance, if you are motivated by personal growth, make sure that the organisation and job will enable you to spend time developing.

▌ Share what motivates and energises you with your boss and colleagues.

As a manager:

▌ Recognise that the same things that motivate you may not motivate your people.

▌ Actively find out what motivates and energises your colleagues, team members and boss.

▌ Incorporate this into coaching and performance review discussions.

Performance management

It is much more difficult to measure non-performance than performance.

Harold S. Geneen, former CEO of ITT

Performance management is about getting the best out of people. It is the process of bringing together the many different elements that make up the practice of managing people effectively. It should be part of the strategic process of any organisation and should be the responsibility of each and every individual in the organisation.

Most organisations have performance management structures and processes which are part of their HR policies and procedures. Line managers, however, have a special role to play in the process as it is their job to manage their people and help them to perform to the best of their ability. It is about creating shared understanding of what is necessary for organisational and personal success. The actual process adopted varies from organisation to organisation, but the important thing is that whatever the approach, it will help you to manage your people effectively if used well.

In order for any performance management process to be successful it must link to and reflect the strategy, goals, culture and style of the organisation. Alignment with these areas is vital to ensure that people know what is expected of them and how what they are doing day to day contributes to the organisation's overall goals and objectives. It is also necessary to be clear about the drivers of the performance management system employed in your organisation. Is it predominantly reward driven, with an emphasis on the delivery of targets and performance-related pay? Or is it development driven, where the emphasis is on ensuring people have the appropriate competences, skills and process for the needs of the organisation? Typically, performance management processes involve elements of both these drivers, but it is worth knowing which predominates as this will affect how you manage your own performance and that of others.

At its best, good performance management in an organisation can contribute towards:

▌ a clear understanding by all of the organisation's vision, strategy and goals

▌ a common culture of commitment and performance

▌ clarity about personal responsibilities and measures of success

▌ excellent communication between and within all areas of the business

▌ a well-developed, engaged and motivated workforce

▌ creating an environment where the organisation provides career development processes and opportunities.

Implementing good performance management processes and practices and ensuring they prevail can be challenging

Implementing good performance management processes and practices and ensuring they prevail can be challenging. So it is worthwhile noting some of the problems that may emerge. These include:

- lack of clarity about the organisation's vision and strategy
- no clear links between the individual's goals and objectives and those of the organisation
- inconsistencies in approach
- rewarding the wrong behaviour
- lack of commitment to the process by managers and individuals
- measurement criteria which are so vague that they are worthless
- no clear process for career development.

As a people leader or manager your role in this process is vital. The first stage for you is to understand the approach your organisation uses. As a leadership and management tool, performance management is probably one of the most important organisational processes for you to master, to enable you to:

- create and manage good quality relationships with your team members
- develop your credibility and reputation
- communicate effectively with your team about organisational goals and objectives
- build a culture of commitment, engagement and motivation
- ensure your people are rewarded, developed and promoted appropriately.

Once you understand your organisational approach it is your responsibility to execute the processes competently and professionally. In order to understand the approach

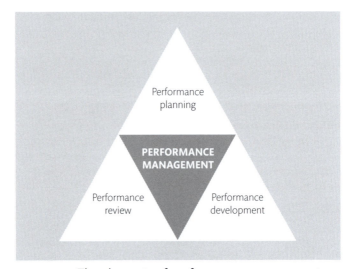

FIGURE 9.1 The elements of performance management

taken you should talk with the relevant people in your HR department who should be able to help you get to grips with the main principles and practices. In addition to this it will be useful to discuss the approach with your boss and colleagues who have to use the system to get their perspective. You should also familiarise yourself with any paperwork and data collection used during the process.

Many performance management systems will involve you in three elements of the process on a regular basis, as illustrated in Figure 9.1.

In essence, your role and responsibility for performance management involves:

▌ *performance planning*, where you work with each individual in your team to establish their main responsibilities, specific goals, objectives and the measures for success

▌ *performance development*, where you are responsible for ensuring your people have the necessary skills and capabilities to do their job and that you understand their career ambitions

▌ *performance review*, which is the continuous process of discussion between a manager and their reports about performance, behaviour, capabilities and progress towards achievement of goals and ambitions.

For any performance management process to be successful it must be fit for purpose and reviewed regularly, and it must adopt systems and processes that are appropriate for the organisation, the type of work done in the organisation and the people who work there. It is very easy for organisations and managers to pay lip service to these processes, but if you want to be regarded as a good leader of people you must take your responsibilities for this area seriously. It is one of the key areas for you to develop and build your credibility – your understanding of the process overall and how it fits into the organisational culture and strategy and then how you use your skill set to manage the processes and effectively engage with your people. Essentially it is a continuous two-way process where each party shares their expectations of the other.

There is a range of tools and techniques that can contribute to your success in this area – we will explore these under the three main areas that you will be involved in as a practising manager who has to manage the performance of colleagues.

It is a continuous two-way process where each party shares their expectations of the other

Performance planning

In recent years there have been shifts in the approaches organisations adopt for managing performance. These shifts are dominated by the move towards a clear relationship between, on the one hand, the organisation's mission, strategy and goals, and on the other hand, personal objectives and key performance indicators. Typically, an individual's objective and key performance indicators will cascade from the overall business objectives. So, as a performance manager you must be aware of your organisation's mission, strategies and goals, and how your own and your team's objectives contribute to the overall business performance. This knowledge and awareness will enable you to have a meaningful conversation when you are discussing an individual's performance targets for the year. This link with the overall business objectives is vital to ensure that process is successful and effective within your organisation.

FIGURE 9.2 The levels of organisational goals

Figure 9.2 indicates the various levels of organisational goals that you should be aware of and it is important that you understand the detail and can see the links at each level.

Once you understand the context it is time to begin discussions with your team members to agree and set their performance targets for the next performance period. This is usually a year, but given the speed of business life today, this is changing, with personal goals flexing during the year to accommodate changes in the business environment. Any goals or objectives set must be:

▌ clearly linked to the priorities of the business and reviewed and updated regularly throughout the year. It is useful to use these goals as a template for any regular meetings you have with your line reports

▌ results oriented and focused on outputs, not activities

▌ specific and measurable, with indicators of what acceptable performance means, or actually looks like

▌ attainable yet challenging enough to stretch and develop the individual

▌ within the context of the role and matched with the individual's skills, experience and development level.

Typically organisations will have protocols for assessing and expressing an individual's performance

It is important that people know how their performance will be assessed in terms of both qualitative and quantitative measures. Measurement is job specific and contextual, though typically organisations will have protocols for assessing and expressing an individual's performance, for instance, the difference between hard and soft measures. Hard measures usually state the output desired, '5 per cent margin on business managed' or 'a 7 per cent increase in annual turnover' or 'build a relationship with six new clients during the year'. Soft measures are more challenging and require some thought about how you describe the level of performance required. For instance, for sales staff you may like to highlight the importance of eye contact, a welcoming smile and a business-like appearance.

Many organisations link these to behaviour displayed by the individual and measured via a competence framework for different roles and different levels within the organisation. These frameworks will identify the competences necessary to be effective in the job and will usually have a range of behavioural indicators that will help you to assess an individual's performance in an area. So, for instance, a telesales person will be measured by the number of calls dealt with and the number of sales made, which are both hard measures, but also by their telephone attitude and manner, which is a soft measure and more difficult to assess. The important thing is to make it clear to the individual what behaviours constitute excellent, acceptable and unacceptable performance.

One word of warning in this area, though. It is often said, 'what gets measured gets done', implying that if something is not measured then it gets ignored. So, for example, if you do not measure a manager's time spent coaching the team, it may fall by the wayside. This is one of the main reasons for some of the criticisms levelled at performance management processes, especially if it is also linked to performance-related pay. This also suggests that the success of any performance management process is largely in the hands of the people who take part in it. Performance planning means that you must pay attention to hard and soft measures, tangible and intangible measures, and attitudes and behaviour – all of these are part of an individual's contribution to the organisation and performance in their role.

Performance planning means that you must pay attention to hard and soft measures

One technique that is becoming increasingly popular is the use of a balanced scorecard approach, where the organisation's and the individual's performance criteria are categorised in the same way – the difference being the actual goals for each department, team and individual. Typically a balanced scorecard would look something like Table 9.1.

TABLE 9.1 Example of a performance balanced scorecard

Organisation Mission/Vision			
Business Strategy for the Year			
Departmental Goals			
PERSONAL GOALS			
Sales Targets	Client Management	Team Relationships	Organisational Contribution

The aim is to illustrate how an individual's goals, objectives and targets relate to the overall goals for both their team and the organisation. This then allows the performance manager and the individual to personalise the goals and targets to suit the person, incorporating soft and hard, tangible and intangible measures, as well as discussing attitudes and behaviours.

Performance development

Good performance management processes ensure that learning and development is ongoing and continuous throughout the year. People should be encouraged to take responsibility for their own development. Your role as their manager is to support them in this and to ensure that you are aware of their needs and wishes, and that appropriate development opportunities are available. One approach is to have a personal development plan (PDP) that is kept up to date and shared and discussed during performance review meetings. There are many other ways of contributing to your own development (some of which are discussed in other chapters – specifically Chapters 3 and 4). The important thing is to ensure that you have the necessary skills and capabilities to fulfil your job role and, if appropriate, to prepare you for promotion.

Performance development is not just about attending training courses. Of course, this is one way of developing yourself, but there are others, including job shadowing, secondment, project work, online learning, coaching, mentoring, reading relevant literature and networking. Development is focused on helping you to be more effective in your current role or it's about preparing you for future possibilities by broadening and deepening your knowledge, skills and capabilities.

Some people are very clear about their development needs, but there are many more who are not. One way of helping people to understand what is necessary for their development is to relate it to the competences necessary for success in their job. Many organisations have developed competence frameworks, which managers can use with their team to help them assess strengths, weaknesses and development needs. Typically, these frameworks are linked to organisational levels or roles and draw upon a range of competences, each with behavioural descriptors that can then be used to assess performance, for instance those in Table 9.2.

TABLE 9.2 Behavioural descriptors used in performance assessment

COMPETENCE	BEHAVIOURAL DESCRIPTORS	PERFORMANCE LEVEL 1 = POOR 5 = EXCELLENT
INFLUENCING	1. Ask open questions 2. Look for common ground 3. Match non-verbal communication 4. Develop relationships 5. Credibility in your subject	

This creates an objective way of looking at a person's overall competence in their role. The addition of asking others for feedback about their skill (popularly known as 360-degree feedback) gives you and the individual themselves an even better review of their development needs. By taking part in such a process you can easily identify areas where you can build on and deploy your existing skills to best advantage and those areas where you need development. Part of the performance management process is to discuss with your manager how you can best develop your skills and how the organisation and your manager can help.

As we said earlier, this isn't just about attending training courses. Recent research undertaken at Ashridge (the Ashridge Management Index 2012) shows that organisations are using a wide range of different approaches, though training courses remain the most popular. Table 9.3 (overleaf) indicates which approaches are used.

TABLE 9.3 Approaches used in personal development

Development approach	Percentage of organisations using this approach for individual development	Percentage of people who have taken part in training in last 12 months
In-company courses run by an in-company trainer	62%	39%
Open enrolment courses provided by external providers	50%	30%
Customised courses provided by external providers	54%	28%
Internal coaching	48%	17%
External coaching	39%	16%
Online learning	54%	33%
Mobile learning	10%	4%
Qualification programmes	48%	13%
Corporate university	16%	5%
Other, including: mentoring, networks, on-job training, action learning, secondments, assignments, shadowing	2%	2%

It is also interesting to note, in the same study:

▌ 57 per cent think that their organisation allocates sufficient time to their learning and development

▌ 73 per cent indicate that in recent years they have spent more time coaching their staff

▌ 78 per cent believe that they would benefit from having a coach

▌ 38 per cent believe there is little support for their development from the organisation

▌ 60 per cent believe that technology has improved learning and development opportunities in the organisation

▌ 58 per cent believe that their organisation wishes to use technology more for learning and development

▌ in most cases, more than 80 per cent of managers believe that whichever learning and development approach is used is effective.

This data suggests that organisations are getting better at providing learning and development opportunities for their staff. However, there is still much room for improvement.

The main point about individual development as part of the performance management process is to ensure that all staff have the opportunity to develop their skills and capabilities and that this process feeds into the organisational learning and development plans and strategies.

Ensure that all staff have the opportunity to develop their skills and capabilities

Performance review

This is the face-to-face meeting you have with your boss and your direct reports. In our view this should be ongoing throughout the year and the rather outdated only once a year performance appraisal should be avoided. In today's fast-changing and complex business environment it is important to have regular meetings to keep up to date – all of these meetings can be seen as part of the performance management process, though some will have a more formal process and structure than others.

We suggest the process shown in Figure 9.3 (or something similar to suit your particular situation), which should be ongoing throughout the year.

In order to get the best from any of these meetings you must also prepare, be fully attentive during the discussion and review/follow up afterwards. In terms of preparation you should establish the agenda with the other party prior to the meeting. This should take account of both your own and the other person's needs. Be clear about the time available and ensure that you have a private meeting space – this

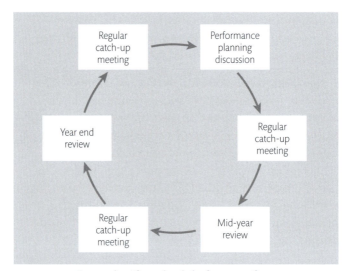

FIGURE 9.3 Example of a schedule for a performance review

is especially important with the prevalence of open-plan offices; go off site if necessary. Finally, make notes about the issues you wish to cover to ensure you get the very best out of each meeting.

You must ensure the meeting is a two-way process where you both ask questions, listen, check your understanding and summarise what you have agreed. You should also be prepared to give feedback and constantly review goals and objectives, taking account of the current situation and climate in your organisation, department or team. These performance discussions should be progressive and deal with what is happening at the time rather than being static and slavishly focusing on goals and objectives that have been overtaken by events.

Once the meeting is over it is important for both parties to review, summarise and do any follow-up, for instance confirming any new goals and objectives, organising any training or development that has been agreed, or simply summarising your meeting to ensure both parties have a clear understanding of what was covered and agreeing the date of your next meeting.

One area of the performance discussion that is often overlooked is the individual's career ambitions. Our research indicates that many people feel that neither their organisation nor their manager offers sufficient support or interest in their career development and ambitions. While we would always suggest that your career and development are largely your own responsibility (see Chapter 2), we also believe that a good leader will always invest time to understand and provide support for the career ambitions of their team members.

By adopting this ongoing review/discussion process you will:

▌ keep vital contact with your team members

- be able to give regular feedback to people, thus ensuring there are no surprises at the more formal meetings
- be aware of their progress towards achievement of their goals
- be able to react to both organisational and personal issues and to take new opportunities and deal with any performance problems as they arise
- provide ongoing coaching (see Chapter 4) using the day-to-day challenges as opportunities for development
- demonstrate your commitment to and interest in your people's performance, development and career future.

The most important element of this ongoing process is that you will be developing a quality relationship with your boss and with your direct reports. As we have already established, successful leaders in today's complex, busy world must invest in their relationship network in order to ensure they can perform and deliver to the best of their ability. Adopting good performance management practices will undoubtedly contribute to your overall success as a boss, manager and leader.

Tips for success

- Link your performance management discussions to the business mission, strategy and goals.
- Be clear about what is expected of your people in order for the organisation to be successful by agreeing specific goals and objectives.
- Sit down with each person and make a specific plan about their contribution to the organisation.
- Provide people with the development opportunities to ensure they have the skills, knowledge and experience to fulfil their responsibilities.

▊ Review on a regular basis to ensure people are on track, know how they are performing against their targets and how what they are doing contributes to the overall organisational goal.

▊ Provide support and encouragement for your team members' career ambitions.

10

Conflict management

Whenever you are in conflict with someone, there is one factor that can make the difference between damaging the relationship. That factor is attitude.

William James, American philosopher and psychologist

Conflict and confrontation at work are a fact of life. Dealing with and handling conflict in the workplace is one of the major challenges many leaders, managers and employees face and in our experience it is one which managers feel ill at ease with. Where people come together to work there will be differences of opinion and perspective, and this is the source of much of what we describe as conflict.

We often hear stories of conflict from participants on our training programmes and frequently the people involved are referred to as 'difficult'. But when the story about the situation unfolds, we often find that, as a third party simply listening to the description of the people involved and the conflict scenario, we can easily see both sides. This has led us to recognise that rather than conflict being caused by difficult people, it is caused by what we experience as difficult or different *behaviour* on the part of others. This behaviour can be from an individual or an organisational perspective.

We believe that learning how to deal with conflict in a constructive and effective way can pay dividends, both individually and organisationally. In this chapter we will explore what causes conflict, both individual and organisational, why it is important to handle it, typical strategies for coping with conflict, and offer you a conflict-resolution process that you can use (and adapt) to deal with your own difficult situations.

> Learning how to deal with conflict in a constructive and effective way can pay dividends

Conflict – a definition and causes

Conflict at work can be defined as any time that disagreement or opposition of ideas and interests arise. There are many causes of conflict, at both an individual and an organisational level.

At an individual level:

- Misunderstanding due to poor communication between people. Often this is related to a person's inability to clearly articulate their needs, or their poor listening skills.

- People with differing values where each person sees the world from their own perspective, for instance people from different professional backgrounds, genders, life stages or cultures.

- Disparate personal interests where the individuals are focused on their own particular needs, goals and objectives.

- Personality clashes where people simply cannot get along.

- Personal problems leading to uncharacteristic behaviour. This often happens if the person is under pressure in their personal life.

At an organisational level:

▌ Poor work environment where management practices are inadequate and unfair.

▌ Rivalry between departments or groups.

▌ Competition for resources between different groups or people.

▌ Organisational financial instability and/or difficult trading environment.

▌ Reorganisation, mergers and joint venture situations.

The impact of these conflicts can be harmful for both the organisation and the individual. From an organisational perspective, conflict can mean that people take their eye off the ball and organisational performance suffers. Additionally, the management and employee trust balance can be adversely affected, with negative consequences for employee engagement and motivation. At an individual level, conflict is stressful and can lead to performance issues. This can ultimately affect your career and your reputation, and others may become wary of dealing with you if they experience you as someone who deals badly with conflict.

Avoiding it does not make the conflict stop or go away

For many of us, avoiding conflict is our preferred strategy, but avoiding it does not make the conflict stop or go away, it simply pushes it to one side for a short time. It will emerge again at some point in the future. Actively confronting issues and handling conflict when it arises will ensure you do as much as possible to contribute to a positive working environment where difference is valued and used effectively for creativity, innovation and growth.

Typical descriptors of difficult people

We have developed this typology based on our experience and the many and varied stories people relate to us about the 'difficult' people in their lives.

▌ The Bureaucrat – usually inflexible, plays it by the rules and won't bend or change, no matter what.

▌ The Logician – someone who theorises all the time, sticking to the objective, rational and logical, doesn't take account of emotion, feelings or mood.

▌ The Deflector – someone who directs attention away from themselves, always asks questions, never commits.

▌ The Finger Pointer – when things go wrong this person always blames other people or processes.

▌ The People Pleaser – someone who wants to be liked above all else and will agree to anything.

▌ The Pessimist – this person is never happy about anything, constantly whines and moans about all aspects of their work and the organisation.

▌ The Bully – someone who is rude, aggressive and negative about others. Never accepts they could be in the wrong and tend to steamroller over others' ideas, opinions and feelings.

▌ The Narcissist – someone who is selfish, vain and self-absorbed. No matter what you are discussing they always take the conversation in the direction of themselves.

▌ The Gossip – someone who talks about you behind your back. Often disguised as the person who knows what is going on but in reality they will often be spreading information and rumour without really knowing whether it is accurate.

Strategies for dealing with conflict

From a strategic perspective there are essentially four strategies that people tend to adopt: avoidance, use of position power, involving third parties or striving for a mutually acceptable outcome.

Avoidance

Avoidance is probably not the best approach as in most circumstances the issue will simply arise again at some point in the future. Avoidance can be experienced in different ways, for instance:

▌ The emotion/feeling suppressor: this is the person who covers up their emotions in service of harmony with others. Often a people pleaser who wants to be liked by others at all costs.

▌ The questioner/topic changer: this is the person who deflects by asking questions or changing the topic of conversation to one of mutual interest or where they know they are aligned, thus avoiding facing the conflict at hand.

▌ The serial avoider: this is the person who avoids conflict at all costs.

When asked why they avoid conflict, people often say it's fear that stops them: fear of hurting the other person, fear of affecting their relationship with the others involved and fear in relation to the response they may get. Others say they simply find conflict too emotionally draining to deal with and it is simply not worth it. They avoid it in the hope it will go away or sort itself out.

Avoidance can be useful on occasions, for instance as a temporary measure to buy time or to let emotions and tempers calm down. It can also be useful if you believe the other party/parties involved may react in a violent or overly aggressive way. Generally, though, avoidance is rarely the answer. It is far better to engage with the issue and attempt to work things through to a mutually acceptable outcome.

> It is far better to engage with the issue and attempt to work things through

Use of position power

The dynamics of a conflict situation can be altered when one party has more power than the other, so it is important to understand the relative distribution of power between the various parties involved in the conflict. Psychologists French and Ravens identified that a person's power can come from different sources:

- Position power – the power inherent within your role: you are the boss, a board member (or similar level person) or your role gives you power over others, for instance you are in charge of health and safety.

- Charismatic power – you are someone people like and don't want to upset.

- Expert power – you have access to knowledge, information and expertise that gives you an advantage over others.

- Coercive power – your force of character makes people fear you in relation to possible recriminations.

- Reward power – you have the ability to incentivise others.

It is always worth assessing the relative power positions of the various people involved in a conflict, including your own, even if they are not going to be used. Forewarned is forearmed and simply knowing who can draw upon what in relation to power is useful information when dealing with any conflict. It is also worth saying that if there is a fairly equal balance of power, then there is a good chance you can work together to sort out the problem without using power plays. However, if there is an imbalance of power, the person with less power may have a challenge on their hands.

Involving third parties

Third-party involvement in conflict situations can be particularly beneficial to support or help the people involved to understand and analyse the situation and then assist them to reach an effective and satisfactory outcome. Third parties are known as facilitators, mediators or, in extremely difficult conflict situations, you may even decide to involve an arbitrator.

When third parties are involved they must be completely independent. Typically they will provide facilitation, process management and discussion intermediary services. The role of the third party is not to solve the issue but to help the parties involved navigate through the process to enable them to reach a mutually acceptable outcome. This means that the third party will do some or all of the following:

▌ meeting organisation

▌ agenda setting

▌ meeting facilitation:

  – listens to both parties' perspectives

  – ensures each person listens to the other

  – clarifies, tests understanding and summarises

  – encourages the disputants to focus on the issues and not on the personalities

> – helps to lead the process to a mutually agreeable
> outcome

▌ prepares a formal written report of the proceedings

▌ formally summarises the outcome.

In certain challenging conflicts there is a formal third-party role called an arbitrator. When an arbitrator becomes involved they act as judge and jury and their role is to listen to both parties' perspectives, review all the paperwork and reach a decision about the outcome.

A mutually acceptable outcome

This strategy is a collaborative strategy for conflict resolution. Both parties work together to reach a mutually acceptable outcome that accommodates each other's needs and objectives. Obviously it is not always possible to adopt this strategy and it usually happens when both parties involved are keen to ensure their current working relationship is maintained. Typically they will have a good level of respect for one another, be equal in relation to power, have a general level of needs and objectives in common, and goodwill. When this strategy is adopted, the parties involved will work together, focusing on the needs and objectives they have in common, and will explore options to work towards a mutually acceptable outcome. We develop this further in the next section.

As a manager or leader of people you may have to deal with conflict under two different circumstances: first, the direct conflicts you face yourself and second, as a boss you may become involved (often as a third party) in the conflict of others. How you manage that process will largely depend upon the strategy you follow. You might find it useful to think back to the most recent conflict situations you have been involved in with either yourself or as a third party.

What strategy did you follow in order to sort things out? With hindsight, might you have dealt with it differently?

When dealing with a conflict, whether it is your own conflict situation or you are involved as a third party, it is helpful to follow a process or at least to use approaches that are supportive in relation to conflict resolution.

A process for conflict resolution

In our last book, *The Leader's Guide to Influence: How to Use Soft Skills to Get Hard Results*, we introduced a five-step process for conflict resolution. We now offer you a seven-step process, which is an adaptation of our earlier work (see Figure 10.1).

Each of the stages involves different skills, approaches and techniques. You can use this process in different ways – you can follow it in stages, starting with Reflect and prepare and

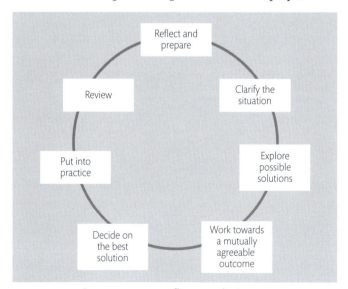

FIGURE 10.1 Seven-stage conflict-resolution process

moving stage by stage to Review, or alternatively you can adapt it by using the stages or even aspects of the stages to suit your particular approach to conflict resolution.

Let's look at what each stage of the process involves.

Reflect and prepare

Be clear about the issue and the people involved. Try to understand your own motives and assumptions in relation to how the conflict/confrontation arose. Reflect on what you hope to achieve in relation to the outcome you desire and the process you wish to adopt in reaching this outcome. Begin to think about how you will handle the actual discussion and be aware that you need a plan. It is important to focus on the issue and not the people, and be aware that becoming overly emotional or being aggressive are two of the resolution killers. Agree with the other parties where and when you will meet to begin the conflict-resolution process – this will be best if it takes place at a time that suits everyone in a neutral and private place.

It is important to focus on the issue and not the people

Clarify the situation

This involves a face-to-face meeting where the vital component is to ask open and probing questions. We find that people tend to jump into the conflict and make assumptions, so asking questions and testing assumptions can be really helpful. It is also important to establish the ground rules (note taking, not interrupting each other, timings, etc.), describe the situation as you understand it and enable the other party to do so as well.

The general rule at this stage is to listen, question for clarification, test understanding and summarise. Both parties should engage in this dialogue and should explain their perspective, including their feelings and ideas for moving ahead.

Explore possible solutions

Brainstorming is useful here to explore all the possible solutions. Brainstorming initially involves withholding judgement until you have the opportunity to fully analyse each of the options and possibilities. Withholding judgement can enable you to come up with creative and new ideas that may lead to innovative solutions that you previously had not considered. Whatever happens during this stage the process will help you to reassess your situation, introduce new ideas and ensure movement by both parties towards a compromise or mutually acceptable solution.

Work towards a mutually agreeable outcome

Once you have brainstormed various possibilities and options for the way ahead, the next stage involves working together with the detail of the various options to move towards a mutually agreeable outcome. Your communication and influencing skills will come to the fore in this stage. Sharing how you feel about the various ideas, questioning and exploring in detail how each will work in reality are key to success. This is a vital stage in the process and having the ability to patiently work through each other's thoughts, ideas and feelings about the various options will indicate that you are listening and willing to compromise on your initial stance. It is really important to be clear and concise, and demonstrate good listening behaviour so that a genuine process of mutual respect is felt. You might like to adopt one of the following active listening processes to help you stay on track:

▌ Three-minute rule – each person has a maximum of three minutes of uninterrupted time to state their views about the issue and ideas for the way ahead. Take it in three-minute turns to speak in a business-like and non-emotional way while the other party is listening and taking notes. You may then find that you begin to appreciate each other's perspective and actually see what you have in common. This in turn can lead to the process of developing a solution. Conflict arises due to misunderstanding and misinterpretation, often caused by poor communication processes. By adopting this rather structured listening and dialogue approach you are forced to listen and reflect on each other's perspectives.

▌ Restating and reflecting – when working towards a mutually acceptable outcome you will probably still be starting from different perspectives. Showing the other party that you are actively listening is a major part of the process for moving ahead. By adopting a process of restating what the other party has said you show them that you are listening and taking on board their disagreement or perspective. So, for instance: *'Jim, I understand that you are annoyed about the decision to downsize the team.'* This approach shows that you have listened and understood, and it provides a platform for moving ahead.

Decide on the best solution

If the previous two stages are carried out effectively you should be beginning to appreciate more about each other's perspectives and differences of opinion as well as identifying possible solutions to the process. This will probably involve compromise on both sides and at this stage it is important to make sure you both clearly understand the detail. Not only is it important to summarise verbally, it is vital to put this in writing and make sure you both agree, having read the notes. So, don't rush this stage, continue to listen, clarify and summarise – closing too quickly without common understanding can lead to reigniting the conflict. Make sure at this stage that you both understand the mutual benefits and consequences of what you have now agreed. For true success, each party should feel that they have contributed to this outcome.

Put into practice

Implementing your solution by putting what you have agreed into practice is the real test, of course. It is now important to observe how this works in practice and for both parties to be willing to work together to ensure success.

Review

Managing conflict effectively is a learning process. It is never easy, involves emotion and usually requires compromise – something many of us find difficult. When you have been successful it is worth reviewing what you actually did to make it happen so that you can build on this approach and also share it with others to help them work with the conflict situations they face at work.

> Closing too quickly without common understanding can lead to reigniting the conflict

What not to do

You should be aware that there are certain behaviours that are unhelpful and should be avoided when dealing with conflict and confrontation:

▌ Getting personal – this is when you take something personally and see all conflict situations as a personal attack or it could be that you attack someone at a personal level.

▌ Using put-downs – this is when you make derogatory remarks about the situation or the person, for instance: *'Well, you would say that, wouldn't you.'*

❚ Being manipulative – by this we mean where one party attempts to use their power or position over the other person or indeed is simply dishonest in terms of the way they handle the situation.

❚ Becoming aggressive – using bullying, shouting, harassing or intimidating behaviour towards others.

Any of the above behaviours will upset, irritate or even anger the other person and will simply serve to fuel the conflict even further.

Conflict and confrontation at work are a fact of business life. Learning how to deal with conflict in a constructive and effective way can be beneficial to both yourself and your business. Avoiding conflict, which is many people's preferred approach, is not an option. Good leaders will adopt a collaborative strategy to work towards a mutually acceptable outcome to any conflict situation.

Tips for success

❚ Recognise that conflict can be healthy as it is simply a difference of opinion which when explored can lead to greater understanding.

❚ Understand your role in the situation – are you part of the conflict or are you managing the conflict between other parties?

❚ Be aware of your normal approach to conflict, how this has served you in the past and how you can continue to develop your approach to dealing with conflict to improve your effectiveness.

❚ Reflect in order to gain a good understanding of the situation and perspectives.

❚ Be aware of people's emotions and how they affect both your own and others' behaviour.

❚ Maintain a professional, issue-based approach.

❚ Review and learn for next time.

11
Relational intelligence

The day is not far off when the economic problem will take the backseat where it belongs and the arena of the heart and the head will be reoccupied by our real problems – the problems of life and human relations.

John Maynard Keynes

We believe that one of the key success factors for any leader or manager is their attitude towards what we call 'relational intelligence'. What we mean by this is 'an individual's full range of interpersonal and intrapersonal intelligences and how they deploy their skills and capabilities to manage their own behaviour and their behaviour when working with others' or, put more simply, 'accepting people for who they are'.

We look at relational intelligence through four different lenses that we feel are important: cultural, emotional, social, political (see Figure 11.1). We believe that understanding these different aspects contributes to a greater awareness, skill and capability in the relational intelligence area.

Our definitions of the four lenses of relational intelligence are as follows:

▌ Emotional awareness is your ability to identify, evaluate, manage and regulate your emotions.

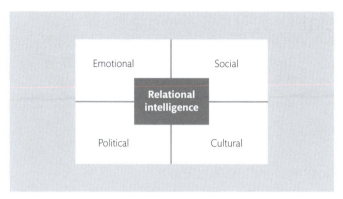

FIGURE 11.1 The four aspects of relational intelligence

▌ Social awareness is the ability to work with others to demonstrate empathy, recognise other people's emotional states and respond accordingly.

▌ Cultural awareness is your ability to operate effectively in diverse and multi-cultural contexts.

▌ Political awareness is your ability to deploy your skills and behaviour to effectively manoeuvre the political landscape in your organisation.

Another way of looking at this is that the emotional and political lenses both relate to you and how you choose to deploy your behaviour, while the cultural and social lenses relate to how you work with others.

Another important element of relational intelligence is that this must be authentic and genuine. In recent years there has been much written about this whole area and many people now recognise the need to be more capable in relational intelligence rather than paying lip service – undoubtedly if this is the case you will be caught out. Truly relationally intelligent people will operate in a skilful, empathetic and genuine way. Those who simply 'take on a role of being relationally intelligent' will find it very hard to keep the charade going for any length of time and will often fall into traps when dealing with others.

> Truly relationally intelligent people will operate in a skilful, empathetic and genuine way

Let's look at each of the lenses and what they involve.

Emotional self-awareness

Daniel Goleman popularised the term 'emotional intelligence' in 1996 when his bestselling book *Emotional Intelligence* was published. However, the term can in fact be traced back much further to R.K. Thorndike who, in 1920, used the term 'social intelligence' to describe the skill of understanding and managing other people. Even further back, Charles Darwin talked about the expression of emotions in his book published in the 1870s, while in ancient Greece the Stoics and the Epicureans believed that the ability to enjoy life was reduced by two major weaknesses: lack of control of the emotions and paying too little attention to the present.

We believe emotional awareness is about developing your ability to:

▌ recognise your feelings and emotions

▌ understand how emotions and feelings affect your mood and state of mind

▌ manage and regulate your emotional state

▌ develop the ability to adjust to and deal with situations in an appropriate way.

A combination of self-awareness, understanding the importance of emotions and recognising the difference between thoughts and feelings will contribute to your emotional awareness. In this context, emotional self-awareness is about getting in touch with your thoughts about the interaction or situation, how it makes you feel, the effect it has on your body responses, your state of mind, and how it makes you behave. One of the most important aspects is to be able to identify and name your emotions and emotional responses to people and situations. To do this it is essential to practise by recognising your emotional responses to various situations and how they make you feel and act.

For instance, you may be very organised and structured in your approach to work and your boss is a last-minute, fly-by-the-seat-of-the-pants type of person. While you find this acceptable much of the time as long as it doesn't have too much impact on your way of working, on other occasions you find it annoying, and you feel he does not respect your way of working, which you find frustrating. An emotionally intelligent person might decide to discuss this with his boss, indicating that *'when he changes his mind and expects you to adapt your approach to his way of working it makes you feel out of control and frustrated and perhaps you could talk about this'*. In situations like this, sharing your feelings is not a sign of weakness, as so many people seem to think, but rather it is demonstrating emotional self-awareness so that you are conscious of each other's needs, which will help you to work most effectively together.

Of course, feelings can express positive emotions as well, so for instance when you feel optimistic, elated or excited about something it is always sensible to share this. Recognising, naming and sharing the full range of your emotional responses will help you to manage many of your relationships more effectively and can also contribute to the process of helping others to understand you.

You may find it interesting to think about your emotions and feelings. To help you in this process, Figure 11.2 gives a range of examples of feeling words.

FIGURE 11.2 Wordle showing examples of feeling words

When you become adept at recognising, naming and sharing your emotions, the next stage of emotional awareness is to manage and regulate your emotional state so that you can deal appropriately with the situation you are facing. So, for instance, you may have had a disagreement with a colleague you find difficult to work with. It would be easy to let your anger get the better of you and say some things you may regret in the future and damage the relationship irreparably. Emotionally intelligent people are more likely to recognise that they feel anger and possibly frustration, but demonstrating this will not help the situation.

A more effective way of dealing with the situation would be to recognise the emotions that you are feeling and then work through how best to get your working relationship back on track, not by denying your emotion but by regulating it and deploying it in a way that both parties leave the situation satisfied with the outcome.

Social awareness

This is the ability to work with others by demonstrating empathy, recognising other people's emotional states and, when interacting, responding appropriately. Most of us have to work with others on a day-to-day basis and for many people maintaining good working relationships is one of the main challenges they face. While emotional awareness is about your own emotional state, social awareness is about developing your ability to recognise and react appropriately to the emotions of others. It is behavioural, interpersonal and action oriented. It is also about timing, knowing when as well as what to say and how to interact with others as well as knowing what *not* to say.

Social awareness depends on your ability to adapt and flex your behaviour in the hope that others will respond accordingly. Socially aware people recognise that they have to:

▌ understand the basis of the relationship – for instance, is it solely work based, is it a personal friendship or is it a combination?

▌ understand their motivation for the interaction and their thoughts, emotions and feelings about the topic

▌ demonstrate empathy by:

  – listening actively to both the verbal and the non-verbal cues and clues as to the other person's perspective about the issue

  – entering into a dialogue by asking incisive and

appropriate questions to demonstrate interest in the other person's perspective

- testing understanding to ensure they are getting to grips with and respecting the other person's thoughts, emotions and feelings in relation to the topic or issue

- tuning into the other person's behaviour and language patterns so that they can respond appropriately

▌ ensure that other people feel they have been listened to and that their views have been respected; that they are sensitive to other people's needs and wants as well as their own.

Social awareness is largely about appreciating others, making time to listen, explore and understand others' perspectives. It is about recognising that we all express ourselves in our own unique way and that successful working relationships demand that you flex your behaviour and emotional responses to build rapport, develop relationships and reach effective outcomes.

Cultural awareness

This is about our ability to operate effectively when dealing with difference, for instance in terms of the main areas of nationality, gender, profession, age, region and organisation. This is not simply about operating across different nationalities but more about recognising the importance of difference and how you respond to it.

On our courses we often find that like-minded groups tend to gravitate towards one another. For instance, it is not unusual to find that all the women on a course sit together for meals, or everyone from a particular country or people from similar professional backgrounds gravitate towards each other.

Similarity means that you have things in common which can make it easier to communicate and operate together.

However, it is difference and how we work with difference that can make things more interesting and is a reality in life. In our context, cultural awareness is about your ability to recognise and operate effectively with diversity. The key issue with cultural awareness is that you instinctively know there is difference in the way you perceive and deal with issues and yet you must accept, recognise and work with that difference in order to operate effectively in most business environments.

> Cultural awareness is about your ability to recognise and operate effectively with diversity

There are a number of skills that are useful when dealing with cultural difference:

▎ Show respect for the other parties.

▎ Be prepared to adapt and be flexible to accommodate other cultures.

▎ Show empathy and develop rapport.

▎ Don't be critical and jump to assumptions.

▎ Recognise that your way of doing things is not the only way.

▎ Ensure everyone has a voice.

The way any person sees the world is affected by their upbringing, the effect of parental influences, other authority figures who have educated and conditioned them and experiences they have during their education and early days at work. So difference is a fact of life. Accepting and recognising difference and deploying your skills and capabilities of emotional and social awareness when you recognise that you are dealing with diversity will contribute to your skill in relation to cultural awareness.

Political awareness

Politics in business is a fact of life. Many people regard political skill as a negative attribute. We believe the reality is that unless you are able to operate within the political landscape in your organisation and business life, you will not be as effective as you could be. Research has shown that lack of political awareness is one of the main derailers for young managers.

Political awareness is about:

▌ working with the informal organisation – getting to know how things are done

▌ knowing who holds the power and influence

▌ knowing how to position yourself and your ideas to best advantage

▌ getting the timing right when presenting new ideas

▌ knowing how decisions are made and who makes them

▌ reading between the lines – not taking things at face value.

Political awareness is about ensuring your goals and objectives are aligned with those of the business. It's about planning and preparing to ensure that you deploy your skills and abilities and demonstrate empathy, tact, respect and understanding for others.

Being politically aware is sometimes seen as negative, particularly if used in a manipulative and selfish manner, when it is often referred to as Machiavellian. We believe that if used to good effect, in a skilful and respectful way, political awareness will contribute to your relational intelligence, success and skill.

The following quiz will help you to reflect and assess your attitude towards and skill in the relational intelligence area.

Relational intelligence assessment

Self-reflection
Look at each statement, score yourself (1 being low, 5 being high), then make notes about how you think you could develop further in this area e.g. what does my score tell me about my attitude and skill in this area of relational intelligence and what can I do to improve?

	SCORE	NOTES
EMOTIONAL		
1 I find it easy to talk about my feelings.	1 2 3 4 5	
2 I recognise when my emotion is affecting my mood.	1 2 3 4 5	
3 I understand that my feelings will impact on my behaviour.	1 2 3 4 5	
SOCIAL		
4 I find it easy to read other people's moods.	1 2 3 4 5	
5 I adapt my behaviour to accommodate others' needs.	1 2 3 4 5	
6 I am aware of non-verbal communication and body language.	1 2 3 4 5	
CULTURAL		
7 I enjoy working with people from other cultures.	1 2 3 4 5	
8 I flex my behaviour to match different contexts and cultures.	1 2 3 4 5	
9 I accept that my beliefs and values are not superior to others.	1 2 3 4 5	

POLITICAL		
10 I understand who holds power in my organisation.	1 2 3 4 5	
11 I know when to make a stand and when to 'shut up'.	1 2 3 4 5	
12 I know who the 'go to' people are.	1 2 3 4 5	

Now reflect about your scores and the notes you made. Identify which of the components of relational intelligence you feel most comfortable with and which you find more challenging. As relational intelligence is a major contributor to any manager's success, you should now identify the key areas that you wish to develop for your particular situation and context.

Relational intelligence is about understanding both your own and others' emotional states and needs.

Tips for success

▌ Take time to focus on and name your emotions in various work situations.

▌ Reflect on your feelings and emotions and how these affect your moods.

▌ Observe others to pick up cues and clues about their emotional states to help you read behaviour in various interpersonal situations.

▌ Practise flexing and adapting your behaviour to get the best out of various situations.

▌ Take opportunities to work in new situations to enable you to develop your breadth of experience and ability to flex your behaviour for reaching effective outcomes.

part

3

Your business

Change

When we are no longer able to change a situation, we are challenged to change ourselves.

Viktor Frankl

As change is both unavoidable and inevitable, any successful leader or manager of people must have a positive attitude to it. This means having both the capability to act as a change agent within their organisation and the ability to help others to deal with change and understand their responses and reactions to it.

In this chapter we will explore the nature of change, attitudes to change, individual and organisational change, resistance and barriers to change, and we will introduce processes and techniques to help manage change effectively.

Types of change

Change affects both individuals and organisations and can be broken down into four segments: planned or emergent change, which is either imposed upon you or initiated by you.

Planned change involves structure and systems where a change is intended to lead to improvements. It is often

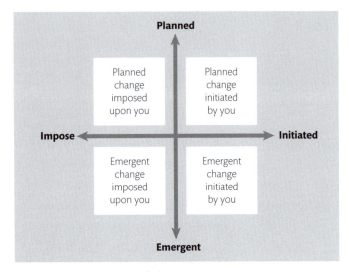

FIGURE 12.1 Typology of change

driven by management and appears to be controllable, with an end goal in mind.

Emergent change is more fluid and ongoing, where change is more of a continuous process. It is messy, involving flexibility and experimentation where the outcome is unpredictable and often surprising.

How individuals and organisations respond to change is undoubtedly affected by whether or not the change has been imposed upon them or initiated by them.

Figure 12.1 illustrates this.

▌ Planned change imposed upon you – this involves structure, system or process changes, which are deemed by management to lead to improvements in business outcomes.

▌ Planned change initiated by you – this involves structure, system or process change that you plan to implement.

▌ Emergent change imposed upon you – the nature of emergent change is such that you cannot predict how and when it will come; rather, it is a fluid ongoing process imposed on you by external forces. This could be environmental, market related, technological, new processes or people related.

▌ Emergent change initiated by you – you are probably a senior manager or in a leadership role and have to be aware of the need to react and respond to constant change. It is a process that is not planned and structured but is initiated by you.

When dealing with change it is beneficial to identify what type of change it is. So, as a leader or manager of people you will have change imposed upon you and you will also be an initiator of change. Clearly, your attitude to any change will be determined to some extent by whether or not you are the initiator. Each one of us has different attitudes to change and the process of change. As the initiator you are most likely to be positive, excited and committed to the change. However, other people may not hold the same views as you and you must accept that just because you are highly motivated about the change, your colleagues may not be. Understanding why resistance exists is an important part of the process of becoming a successful change agent.

> Each one of us has different attitudes to change and the process of change

Resistance to change

Some degree of resistance is always to be expected as change will almost certainly be unsettling and stressful for all of those involved – the change agent included.

So, why do people resist change? Here are some of the most common reasons for individual resistance:

▌ Fear of the unknown – which could be lack of awareness of the need for change, fear of new systems, people, processes or lack of training and skill to operate effectively during and after the change.

▌ Complacency – things feel comfortable and secure as they are with well-established habits which will be difficult to change.

▌ Insecurity – a general feeling of losing out and fear about the future for your job.

▌ Lack of understanding – little knowledge of the need for or purpose of the change. This is usually related to poor communication and information by the instigators of the change.

▌ Self-interest – a selfish focus on how the change will affect the individual themselves. Often related to position power or perceived effect upon salary and reward.

▌ Disagreement with the planned change – no buy-in to the change or disagreement about the process, timing, advantages and disadvantages of the change.

In addition to these individual resistors there are several common organisational barriers, including:

▌ the reputation of previous change programmes in the organisation, especially when there has been a track record of failure

▌ poor management in introducing the change to the organisation – no explanation of the need for change, no consultation or involvement of people in the process, and no evidence of training or development to deal with the change

▌ power structures within the organisation, where senior and influential people put up barriers to any change.

These resistors will all have an effect upon an individual's attitude to change and whether or not they embrace or resist change. People's behaviour in relation to change has been the subject of much research and theorising and there are two models for change which help to categorise people's attitudes/feeling about change and might help you to understand your particular responses.

For instance, Fiona was part of a small group responsible for instigating a planned change at Ashridge. The change involved asking faculty to change offices. The rationale behind the change was to bring faculty together into one building to encourage greater communication, sharing and community. The instigators were extremely surprised to find that many people responded in an emotional way and in general people were resistant.

On reflection, the reasons for this resistance were:

▌ lack of understanding about the reason for the change

▌ lack of consultation.

In our excitement about the benefits of this change, we failed to consider our colleagues' views and needs. How could we have avoided it? In fact, it was very simple: we should have talked to people, shown an understanding of their emotional response, tried to get their buy-in before instigating the change, and helped them understand the reason for the move.

You may find it useful to reflect on various change processes you have been involved in. In the first instance, think about times when you have initiated the change. What kind of change was it – planned or emergent? Now think about any resistance you experienced from colleagues. What type of resistance was it and why do you think it came about? How could you have dealt with it differently to avoid this resistance?

Second, when you have had change imposed upon you, what kind of change was it – planned or emergent? Now think about how it made you feel. Did you feel any resistance? Try to describe it and the reason why. What could have been done differently to remove your resistance?

Models of change

The Swedish psychologist Dr Claes Janssen created the Four Rooms of Change model based on his research into how people experience change, which started in 1964 and continues today with Ander & Lindström Partners Consulting AB. The model looks at what happens with people and organisations in change and helps you to measure people's attitudes to change, the organisational climate and readiness for change.

Dr Janssen's theory suggests that during the change process individuals and organisations alike go through a journey which starts with contentment, moves through denial into confusion and finally, if we are lucky, into renewal. Dr Janssen points out that we have to go through this cycle, that we cannot skip from contentment to renewal.

Successful change management involves navigating through all four rooms in order to effectively bring about change. Organisations that fail to do this can and do fail when they don't deal effectively with denial or confusion, and there are many examples of companies ceasing to exist when this happens. For example, some of the recent failures in both the financial services and retail sectors can certainly be put down to avoidance of dealing with each of the stages of the change process.

Successful change management involves navigating through all four rooms

A brief description of what happens in each room follows. However, for a fuller description of this and how to use the model we suggest you visit Dr Janssen's website (www.claesjanssen.com).

In the contentment room you find people (or organisations) who reflect on past glories and have become complacent, relying on the fact that what got them to where they are today will continue to succeed in the future. Those stuck in complacency must go through denial and confusion before they can move to renewal.

In the denial room, as its name suggests, there is a refusal to acknowledge that any kind of problem exists, even though it is rather obvious to colleagues and customers. While a person or company is in denial there is no chance that they can move on until they accept the reality of the situation, which can be uncomfortable and hence the tendency to be in denial.

In the confusion room, people accept the issue or change but don't yet know how to deal with it. This leads to doubt, anxiety and uncertainty, which are often characterised by a desire for resolution, which can lead to premature decisions and actions. The confusion room is the place for reflection, development and creativity. It is important to allow people to spend time 'not knowing' and reflecting together on solutions.

In the renewal room, people and organisations have a renewed sense of energy, purpose and commitment. The idea here is to try to keep yourself or your organisation in renewal as long as possible. The reality, however, is that most people and organisations drift back to contentment eventually. This suggests that change is a neverending process, and good managers and leaders must always be aware of the changes affecting their environment.

We have discovered that many managers find this process to be practical and easy to apply to their own change issues. For example, Nigel Melville finds it a particularly valuable tool for change.

William Bridges has an extremely interesting and, we believe, useful and practical theory of change. He believes that change doesn't start with the new, with what is being changed, but rather with the old, with what is ending. His model explores change as a three-step process, starting with what is ending, then moving on through what he calls the neutral zone, before coming to what we normally see as the change itself, new beginnings.

What he suggests is that too often we ignore what people are losing in a change process, what is actually ending for them, whereas our focus as managers tends to be on what is beginning. If we can help people end things well, then we are in a better position to deal with change. This involves accepting that people will lose something, that these losses may be subjective rather than objective. They are nevertheless real and people will mourn what is ending as frequently they have an emotional attachment to the past. We have to learn to respect people's need to take a piece of the past with them – this could be symbolic or real.

> If we can help people end things well, then we are in a better position to deal with change

The neutral zone is similar to the confusion room in the Four Rooms of Change model. Bridges, like Janssen, believes that there will be a period of transition and confusion before the change is fully accepted, and that this is perfectly normal. Too often the instigators of change ignore this natural process and expect people to just accept any change without going through a transition. They don't seem to understand that change involves an emotional reaction and observe that many leaders and managers are incapable of dealing with this. Transition is a difficult period in which people need support and systems to help them. It can also be an extremely creative time, when ideas can flourish.

Finally, we come to beginnings. The key aspect here is that as a manager you cannot force people to change, rather you must encourage and support them. Involvement is a prerequisite for successful change, so it is important to give people a role and a part to play. The role of the people manager is that of a facilitator rather than a director of change.

Key themes of change

Recent research undertaken at Ashridge indicates that 75 per cent of the respondents regarded leading or managing change as part of their role. However, it is worrying to note that the same respondents also felt that less than 50 per cent of their organisation's leaders had the skills to lead change well, and only 41 per cent felt that leaders

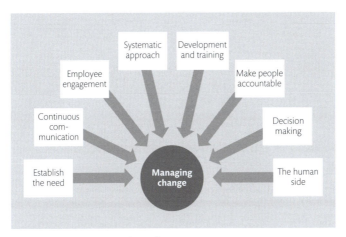

FIGURE 12.2 Change: key themes

were trained to lead change well. This lack of skill and development will undoubtedly account for some of the resistance to change.

Based on this research we have identified the themes in Figure 12.2, which are key to managing successful change programmes.

Establish the need for the change and the desired outcomes

Statements like 'It would be much easier if we all knew and understood where we were going' are commonplace when talking to people about change. In our research, one of the most commonly mentioned problems is the lack of clarity around the need for change. So, no matter what the change is, be it a major organisational change or a minor process change in a department or team, make sure you can clearly articulate the need for change and the desired outcomes.

Any change risks being unsettling for people, but if they have an idea of the vision and are aware of the need for change, trust will be built and people will be more on board with the change process. In addition to establishing the need for change, if you are able to communicate your emotional feelings, define the business benefits and translate these into deliverables, you will add to your reputation as a successful change agent.

Continuous communication during the process

Successful change does not happen quickly and one of the biggest frustrations expressed by people is the lack of communication during the process. Often change is initially heralded by a lot of noise, then things go very quiet, which causes people to feel unsettled, insecure and uninvolved.

Regular updates about the process of change should be given using techniques such as:

▌ walking the talk

▌ corridor meetings

▌ podcasts

▌ 'town hall meetings'

▌ road shows

▌ email.

These will all help keep people in the know. Regular communication will also provide a platform for sharing the benefits as they happen and enabling celebrations for any successes. In addition to this it is important to ensure that senior management and other change agents are accessible and show willingness to engage in dialogue and answer questions throughout the change process. The more people know about the change, the more they feel involved and thus committed to the new ideas.

> The more people know about the change, the more they feel involved

Employee engagement

Change does not have to be top down. Engaging with your people to involve them in the whole process will help to engage people in the journey and get their buy-in. It is important to understand that change happens *with* people, not *to* people, so taking time to involve people at all levels can pay huge dividends. Communication, as mentioned earlier, is of course the key here – in general we can say the more communication, the better employee engagement will be.

Systematic approach to change

Adopt a systematic approach to the change. In our research, phrases such as '*knee jerk*', '*headless chickens*' and '*change for the sake of it*' were often mentioned in conjunction with frustrations about the lack of structure in relation to the process adopted. Having a clearly defined process will help people feel more confident about the change and can reduce frustrations which lead to insecurity and uncertainty. People also talked about having a need for frameworks, setting targets, goals, timeframes, prioritising, reviewing and evaluating as part of the process.

Development and training

This should be implemented for all levels of staff. Our research suggested that investing in people's development signalled a real commitment to the need for change. Many managers are technically competent in their professional area but that does not mean that they are capable or knowledgeable about the skills and processes of change, and how change affects people in the organisation. In terms of training and development, some of the following ideas are important:

▌ Ensure that the people leading the change have the skills and abilities for success.

▌ Offer people coaching – not just managers but all levels of staff. Encourage managers to adopt a coaching approach with their staff so that they are supporting them through the change.

▌ It is especially important to train people in the soft skills. Help them to understand their own and others' attitudes and feelings about change and how change impacts on people. Understand the psychological effects of change and how best to help people through the process.

▌ Develop a change toolkit which can be shared with
everyone, possibly using online techniques to ensure
as many people as possible have access to at least some
training.

Make people accountable

It appears that for many people lack of accountability
for change is a key issue. Our research showed that
nearly 90 per cent of respondents felt that leading or
managing change was a significant aspect of their role
and responsibilities. Yet many mentioned that it wasn't
part of their key performance indicators. Making people
more responsible by setting targets and goals and holding
people to account for delivery of the new ideas will lead
to greater commitment to change. In addition to this,
rewarding and recognising success in achieving the goals,
as well as effort and behaviour change, will improve
people's attitudes.

Decision making

Making clear decisions during periods of change can be
difficult. This is especially so when dealing with emergent
change as it often involves a leap of faith based on what
you believe to be the best way ahead. Clearly, the more
you communicate, consult and plan during the process,
the easier this will be. Tough, unpopular and difficult
decisions are part and parcel of the change process and often
involve such issues as redundancy, reallocation of roles
and cost-cutting exercises. Recognising people's emotional
needs and feelings about change will help you to adopt an
approach to decision making that is appropriate for the type
of decision being made. By this we mean that if you are
dealing with a decision that is clear-cut, obvious and has
little impact on people, then the decision can be quick and

clear. However, if the decision affects people, the way of making and communicating that decision will require more delicate handling and consideration.

> Tough, unpopular and difficult
> decisions are part and parcel of the
> change process

The human side

Possibly the biggest criticism people have about change is the apparent lack of consideration for the human side. When commenting on his experience of change, one manager we interviewed recommended that you treat people '*not as a dispensable resource but as a source of creativity and innovation to help the organisation succeed*'. You ignore the human side of change at your peril. Your people can buy in and make the change happen or alternatively can resist change and constantly put obstacles in the way.

Change isn't easy, so by recognising your own and others' feelings about change, adopting some good management principles and applying common sense you will find the whole process runs more smoothly.

There are many writers and consultants who will offer you their successful change model or process. What we would like to suggest is that change is constant and we all have to adapt, develop and change in order to survive, so being aware of your own attitude or readiness to change, and following some key principles on a day-to-day basis, you will become more confident and capable when leading and managing change.

Try the following self-reflection questionnaire.

Self-reflection questionnaire: My attitude to change

Look at each of the statements and score yourself using the scale 1 to 10, with 1 being a disagreement and 10 being agreement.

	Assessment questions	Score
1	I believe I could improve the approach to my job to be more efficient	1 2 3 4 5 6 7 8 9 10
2	I am open to change any aspect of my role and responsibilities	1 2 3 4 5 6 7 8 9 10
3	I volunteer and look forward to being involved in change projects	1 2 3 4 5 6 7 8 9 10
4	When changes are suggested I willingly embrace them	1 2 3 4 5 6 7 8 9 10
5	I am constantly looking for new ways of doing things	1 2 3 4 5 6 7 8 9 10
6	I lead and take ownership of change projects	1 2 3 4 5 6 7 8 9 10
7	I believe change is beneficial to both the organisation and the individual	1 2 3 4 5 6 7 8 9 10
8	I enjoy learning new things	1 2 3 4 5 6 7 8 9 10
9	I understand my role in making change happen	1 2 3 4 5 6 7 8 9 10
10	I believe I have the right skills, abilities and attitudes to change	1 2 3 4 5 6 7 8 9 10
	Total score	

Basically, the higher your score, the more change ready you are. However, that said, you will need to be aware of your readiness in relation to those you are leading or managing. One of the biggest challenges in managing change effectively is ensuring that the people involved are at a similar level of readiness. If you are all gung ho and excited about a change and your team is sceptical and uncertain, then you will hit hurdles along the way. So, you can also use this brief questionnaire to assess your team's readiness. Once you know this you can assess your next steps, the stage you are at, the stage others are at and the gap between the two. Then you can assess how best to engage and involve the others around you.

Change is a key fact of life. All managers and leaders must learn to deal with, manage and lead change effectively.

Tips for success

▌ Follow a structured process that works for your context.

▌ Communicate early and often – you cannot over-communicate during change processes.

▌ Plan, consult and engage with all stakeholders.

▌ Be open and honest to build trust.

▌ Be clear about what you expect from people during the change process.

▌ Make people accountable for specific actions.

▌ Build change accountabilities into the performance management process.

▌ Be aware and sensitive to the emotions people will be feeling during change and respond accordingly.

▌ Recognise the importance of soft skills in the process.

▌ Develop a toolkit for change and offer training.

■ It doesn't have to be top down – involve everyone.

■ Identify change champions who are there to help others.

■ Be aware that your view of change may not be shared by
everyone.

Derailment 13

Derailment doesn't come out of the blue, striking at a whim. In most cases, it can be predicted, and is usually the responsibility of both the individual manager and the organisation.

Don W. Prince, Center for Creative Leadership

One of the key risks for you to be aware of as a people manager is the risk of derailment. That is to say, the risk of either you being derailed or your people being derailed. So, what do we mean by derailment? It means being knocked off your planned course, of not achieving what you, and others such as your friends, family, manager and HR department, for example, thought and expected you to achieve. But does it happen a lot? Well, studies by US researcher Morgan McCall and the Center for Creative Leadership have shown that derailment is a very common occurrence among high-potential managers in organisations. What happens is that the qualities which initially led these managers to being on the fast track actually have a flip side, which has the potential to knock them off course later in their career.

Sources of initial success

Some of the sources of initial success – and you may well recognise these as qualities you have – are:

▍ good track record – people who get excellent bottom-line results and have high impact in functional/technical areas

▍ brilliance – managers who were perceived as extremely smart and intelligent

▍ commitment/sacrifice – managers who were seen as loyal to the organisation, who were willing to work long hours and accept any assignments. McCall mentions people who worked long hours, seven days a week

▍ charm – people who are seen as charismatic and pleasant

▍ ambition – people who are energetic, high achievers, results focused and want to get on.

The darker side of strengths

But the strengths and qualities listed above can have their dark sides. The strength becomes overdone and then becomes a potential flaw. Let's look at the list of strengths and qualities again and identify some of the potential downsides.

Track record

People may well have a good track record, but that success might often have been achieved in a very narrow area. For example, if it was in a purely technical area, it could have blinded people to the broader context. Success may also have been achieved in destructive ways. Maybe the track record of success was solely down to events such as a rising market rather than the qualities of the person. Or perhaps other people may have had more influence on the success than the executive in question, perhaps it was due to the brilliant

team they had, who were not given credit. Maybe the
executive moved too fast for consequences of their actions to
catch up with them, moving on at just the right time.

So if you are managing people who have an excellent track
record, make sure that none of the above applies to them.

Brilliance

It might seem like an excellent thing to have a brilliant
person, but that too has its downsides. Brilliance can
intimidate others, and brilliant people can devalue people
they see as less brilliant than themselves.

They can devalue others' ideas and contributions because they
are too egotistical. So if you are managing a brilliant person,
what can you do? First, pay close attention to how they interact
and relate with others around them. Are they able to involve
and listen to others? Can they bring other people into the
discussion and recognise good ideas apart from their own? If
they can't then you need to be able to step in and coach them
on this as they may be showing the initial signs of derailment.

> Brilliance can intimidate others, and
> brilliant people can devalue people they
> see as less brilliant

Commitment

Again at first glance it seems that high commitment is a good
thing. But it too has its downsides. Over-commitment can lead
to defining one's whole life in terms of work and then expecting
others to do the same. It can lead to a manager being willing
to do almost anything to succeed, including questionable or
unethical activities. Managers who are too highly committed
may then start to treat their staff badly and use their people
as a means to securing their personal targets. Now, while you

probably don't want to stop people working hard, you might want to pay attention to their work–life balance and ensure that they won't burn out or, worse still, burn others out.

Charm

The downside of charm is that it can be used selectively to manipulate people. And the people who do that are not charming to everyone but are capable of being charming one minute then a dictator the next. So it can be quite hard to spot the negative aspect here. If you do have someone who uses charm a lot, make sure that they are actually being charming to most of the people, most of the time. Let's face it, they are probably going to be charming to you, their boss. Just make sure you know what's going on elsewhere.

Ambition

This is positive, but to be too ambitious is to risk overstretching oneself and the organisation. These managers become unrealistically ambitious and end up taking on more than they can deal with. For instance, British chef, restaurant owner and TV personality Gordon Ramsay said in a newspaper interview that the reason his New York restaurants failed was that he had become too ambitious.

This means that as an effective leader of people you need to be aware of your potential shadow side, in order to be able to manage it. Additionally, be aware of the potential derailers that might affect your team.

Dynamics of derailment

There are three key points that you need to remember when thinking about people's potential to be derailed:

▌ Strengths can become weaknesses.

▌ Blind spots matter eventually.

▌ Success can lead to arrogance.

Strengths become weaknesses

Successful people can become arrogant and overconfident. It becomes difficult for managers to abandon what worked in the past. So in some cases where the context and situation change, for example in a new job or department or in an overseas assignment, their strengths don't change and flex according to the context. Thus they become inflexible, and a strength such as decisiveness can turn into a weakness and be seen as being dictatorial rather than decisive. Technical strength, for example, can lead to micro-management, where instead of coaching and managing you start doing the job yourself, and telling others exactly how to do it. Strong belief in principles can evolve into fanaticism or imposing one's beliefs on others.

> Strong belief in principles can evolve into fanaticism or imposing one's beliefs on others

One manager reported to us that some managers in his organisation were '*so busy doing everyone else's job that they didn't do their own*'. This is an extremely common situation, where managers have been promoted solely on the basis of their technical know-how and ability.

Let us give you an example. Being a tactical genius is great in a situation that calls for tactical skill, but the danger is that this person is unable to adapt to one that calls for strategic awareness and is too preoccupied with details. They then fail to see the bigger picture, are not viewed as strategic and this ultimately leads to them being derailed.

Technical expertise is another strength that is effective in many leadership situations, especially at lower management levels. If, however, a manager's greater technical expertise leads to them over-managing and telling people how to do their jobs rather than letting them get on with their work in their own way, it can become a liability.

This tendency is especially self-destructive when the people being over-managed actually know more about what they are doing than their boss does. This is a frequent occurrence. One manager in a French multinational company admitted that his weakness was his inability to step back and not interfere. His concern was to ensure success, but his inability to let go was having the opposite effect. He didn't give his people a chance to step forward and take responsibility and they ended up resenting him.

Sooner or later, if you are successful, you will end up managing people and functions outside your area of expertise. And then if you want to continue being successful you have no choice but to step back and let go.

People who over-manage can be guilty of:

▌ meddling in things they don't understand

▌ alienating people whose help they need

▌ making mistakes because they won't listen to experts

▌ not getting help from people who are experts because the experts have been alienated for too long and now don't want to help the manager

▌ getting mired in details

▌ not thinking broadly.

Blind spots matter eventually

According to the research, insensitivity is the most common flaw among derailed executives and is the strongest differentiator.

Power and intimidation can produce compliance but insensitivity to others can lead to:

▌ lack of support at crucial junctures

▌ failure of subordinates to pass on important information

▌ active sabotage

▌ loss of ideas from below

▌ other counterproductive activities.

The reason that formerly benign flaws become lethal is usually a change in context. Talented people tend to change situations. Often, for example, they win promotion, get put on development assignments, are given increased responsibilities, and move into new and more visible settings. Then they have a new boss, new demands, a new national culture if they have been assigned overseas, a new organisational culture and so on. These new situations challenge the continued success of a person's particular pattern of strengths and weaknesses. If they find themselves in a situation which no longer plays to their strengths, they are left with only their weaknesses to draw on.

The critical factor is the magnitude of the differences between what went before and what the new situation demands. If we look at Shakespeare's play 'Macbeth' we see that the idea of derailment happened even then. Macbeth was a successful warrior but incapable of being a king. His strengths were in being brave and warlike, not in being a leader who might have to use diplomacy, lead people in peacetime and be capable of restraint.

Macbeth was a successful warrior but incapable of being a king

Boundary jumps also hold a big threat – if you change
functional areas, for instance, or move from one business to
another within an organisation, or move from a line position
to a staff position. People who were previously successful
with an autocratic style have to learn to move to another
style when the territory they operate in has changed.

So what does this mean for the evaluation of managers? It
may be that the traditional fixed template of competence
boxes that get ticked annually might not be of much use.
Reality is much more complex and any evaluation of
competences should surely take account of the context
and how the interaction between a person's strengths and
weaknesses plays out in reality. Don't just look at people's
results, look into how they get the results.

Therefore one must be aware of these strengths and
weaknesses and we can no longer define effectiveness purely
in terms of results. That idea only masks development
needs from both the manager and the organisation. The
organisation is generally keen for results, and rightly so.
It looks at the what and not the how. That is to say that it
looks at what is done, but in doing so it often overlooks the
way in which these results are achieved. And the way in
which results are achieved is clearly important, as it might
lead to longer-term failure. If you are not careful and end
up ignoring your people's weaknesses, or indeed rewarding
them, you are setting the stage for their derailment.

Success leads to arrogance

Arrogance can be present at all levels and is a key feature of derailers. People become out of touch. Arrogance has special features: it grows over time, it creates a feeling of invincibility and a blindness to one's impact and its potential consequences. Arrogance leads to over-optimism. Arrogant managers believe that expertise in one area makes them experts in others.

Arrogance also creates the belief that normal rules do not apply. A relentless pursuit of results without regard for people or values leads to temptation. A high degree of power over others, together with a track record of success, blinds many executives to the reality of their dependence on others. The fact is that you can't do it alone.

So, why don't people correct their weaknesses before they cause problems? The research tells us that there are several reasons, but the main one is that the person has not yet been negatively affected by these weaknesses. We would add that they are perhaps not yet aware, or only partially aware, of these weaknesses. They refuse to admit to any weaknesses and disregard any information and feedback coming to them. They are, in effect, in denial. Their culture, whether national or organisational, may also play a part. So it is important that you develop a high degree of self-awareness, that you as a manager have the strength and energy to give feedback to such a person, that the organisation itself has a robust enough culture to confront this denial, and that support and development – perhaps in the shape of coaching or mentoring – are available.

It is important that you develop a high degree of self-awareness

Learning is essential in the quest to prevent derailment, but unfortunately it is often overlooked in favour of action. Stopping to reflect and learn from a particular course of action is often seen as a waste of time. As McCall says: '*Quite often the real learning from a challenging experience waits for a reflective time after the maelstrom, when what was done wrong and what was done right can be examined in the light of feedback and outcomes. Unfortunately, and especially where talented people are concerned, the reflective period rarely exists.*'

So it is important that you take the time to reflect and above all learn from events.

What can you do to prevent derailment?

It is your job as an effective people manager to make sure that you pick up the signs of potential derailment in your people, and that you have the skills to do something about it. Here are some guidelines:

- *Intervene.* Don't do nothing. Have the courage to intervene and point out the consequences of people's actions.

- *Coach people.* Being a people manager implies that you need to be able to coach and develop your people. See Chapter 4 for more information on how to coach effectively.

- *Give regular feedback.* Don't wait for annual appraisals. Make sure your feedback is frequent so that you catch issues before they get out of hand. Learn how to give feedback effectively and skilfully.

- *Analyse.* Look at your own and others' strengths and weaknesses and list the potential flip sides of your strengths. Be honest with yourself and think about the implications of any overdone strengths.

▌*Have a jester.* In literature you will notice that many kings had jesters, a servant who was allowed to criticise them because no one else would dare to. Make sure you have a trusted colleague who can give you real and honest feedback. Encourage others to challenge you and to tell the truth.

▌*Stop trying to control everything.* Life is complex and uncertain and you can't control everything – so don't try. Allow others space to take initiatives and learn to trust your people more.

▌*Rely less on purely technical skills.* Listen more, tolerate ambiguity more, get more feedback from colleagues and co-workers and external people rather than bosses.

▌*Become more problem-solving focused.* Focus less on promotion.

▌*Become more emotionally aware and intelligent.* We believe that emotional and relational intelligence is often overlooked by many managers. But the ability to connect emotionally and relate to other people is clearly essential to being an effective people manager.

▌*Be aware of your interpersonal impact on others.* Get feedback often. Be prepared to admit to any mistakes, be humble enough to offer apologies for them and make sure you learn from any mistakes.

Derailment and transitions

Most managers and leaders make a number of transitions in their career. Professor Michael Watkins in his 2012 *Harvard Business Review* article suggests several different types of transition without which, he believes, the person risks not being successful. In other words, they are at risk of derailing.

Some of the shifts we have noticed are as follows:

▌ *Specialist to generalist.* An obvious shift but one that is more difficult than it seems. It means letting go of the specific knowledge that you have acquired and the sense of comfort that this knowledge brings. What makes it worse is that you give up knowing stuff and in exchange you get … not knowing! This is an extremely uncomfortable transition.

▌ *Tactician to strategist.* You will have to shift from tactical thinking to a much more strategic perspective. You cannot just look at things from your own, or your team's or even your department's, perspective any more. Again you will have to let go of skills and a mindset it has taken you years to acquire.

▌ *Bricklayer to architect.* You need to move from doing it yourself, and getting the satisfaction from doing that, to making sure it gets done – and gets done properly – by others. This is a whole new ball game and requires both a skill set and mindset.

▌ *Warrior to diplomat.* Your energy, commitment and sheer hard work got you results and probably also promotion. But in the transition you now need to let go of these qualities and become more of a diplomat. You have to learn how to stand back and try to see other people's perspectives. You need to stay in control and not show anger or negative emotions.

As you progress from technical specialist to general management and on to a leadership position, for example, you will surely experience one or more of these shifts. How prepared are you? What can you do to avoid the traps and ensure that you don't derail? As a manager you will need to be aware of people who are going through these transition periods, and ensure that they have both the necessary information about the traps involved and the necessary skills and attitudes to avoid falling into them.

> ## What can you do to avoid the traps and ensure that you don't derail?

Organisational derailment

In 'The Toxic Triangle' in his book *The Elephant in the Boardroom*, Professor Adrian Furnham lists the scenarios where organisational derailment is likely to happen. The ideal scenario for derailment is when there is a dysfunctional leader, coupled with susceptible followers and an organisational culture that allows or encourages paranoia and lacks checks and balances. A dysfunctional leader is one who relies too much on personal power and charisma and who is narcissistic. You may very well have known such a leader. Susceptible followers are those who have low maturity and weak values, together with high ambition and conformity. Organisational cultures which lack checks and balances are unfortunately all too prevalent, as the recent scandals involving the UK National Health Service and Banks in the UK and US demonstrate.

When you have a combination of all three, it's likely that the organisation or unit will derail.

There are, of course, many examples where organisations have failed, including Enron, WorldCom and Barings Bank, for these reasons. Other organisations, like banks, have not failed completely but have had to undergo major reforms or pay huge fines because they have all but derailed.

As a people manager you need to be able to keep an eye open for people who might be becoming too egotistic, people who conform too easily and don't challenge, and be aware also of the prevailing culture of the unit, department or organisation, especially in difficult times.

Derailment is a risk for all of us. With this in mind you may find it beneficial to reflect on some key strengths and how these could be overdone, potential weaknesses and their implications, and finally actions that you could take to modify your behaviour to avoid derailment. Look at the exercise on derailment reflection in Table 13.1.

TABLE 13.1 Derailment reflection

My main strengths are:	If overdone it might appear as:
My weaknesses are:	The implications of these are:

Actions to take to avoid potential future derailment:

This exercise will help you to pre-empt some of your potential derailers. By thinking about your strengths and how you could overdo them you will be more aware of situations where this might happen and be able to adapt your behaviour accordingly. Similarly, thinking about your weaknesses and how they may let you down will enable you to focus on those that you believe are important to develop to prevent future derailment.

The key thing to remember is that not all people who derail show the signs described above, and not all people who do show the signs will derail. Other factors play a part as well. But people who show several of the signs, over a long period of time, are at a much higher risk.

You need to be aware of the fact that there is a transition to be made from specialist to manager and from manager to leader. This applies to your own development and career, but also to those you are responsible for. We have listed the actions you can take above in the section called 'What can you do to prevent derailment?'. Keep these in mind.

Tips for success

▌ Pay attention to transition periods in your career.

▌ Get and act on feedback.

▌ Focus on your people, not your own ambition.

▌ Develop your relational intelligence.

▌ Be aware that all your strengths can have potential downsides.

Positive leadership behaviour

A pessimist sees the difficulty in every opportunity, an optimist sees the opportunity in every difficulty.

Winston Churchill

You will probably have heard of the concept of positive psychology, but how can it help us to become better people managers? Research has shown that using a positive approach can bring benefits both in personal and work relationships and in team performance. There are a number of tools and techniques that we can borrow from this field and they can easily be applied in our daily work as effective leaders of people. We will discuss how to be appreciative, how to respond constructively to others and the four approaches to a solution-focused way of leading people.

How to be appreciative

Being positive and showing appreciation to your people might not come naturally to most managers. As one manager said to us when we shared the concept with him, '*It sounds kind of pink and fluffy to me!*' That is a fairly typical response when we introduce managers to concepts such as appreciative enquiry, positive psychology and the solution focus approach, which are all focused on being appreciative and solution focused rather than problem focused.

We know that showing appreciation to others is a fundamental aspect of being an effective people manager and in developing effective relationships. The need to be valued and appreciated is a basic human need, and if you are to get successful performance from your people, you too need to be able to grasp the basic psychology of appreciation.

Traditionally managers use what we might call a deficit model when dealing with situations at work. That is to say that they assume that things are a problem and that they need to fix the problem. So they get into the habit of focusing on what is going wrong and what is not working, and then trying to fix it. This approach is not just limited to business. In the field of psychology there seems to be a focus on what is wrong with a person and what is not going well. It tends to look at fixing a person's problems and correcting weaknesses. However, increasingly nowadays the idea that psychology should be equally interested in what is going well is gaining ground because some things must be going well for a person, even if other things are not.

How does this apply to relations at work and effective people management? If you have a problem with someone, it is easy to amplify the problem and apply it to everything they do, leading to the other person becoming labelled as a 'problem' person. Many of the managers we work with come to us asking for help in dealing with problem people. But what if the other person is not a problem? After all, they probably don't describe themselves as a problem person! And what does it do to the relationship between you and the other person if you are already labelling them as a problem? How would you feel if your boss was describing you as a problem?

The effective people manager would do two things:

▌ They would focus on the relationship and the issue, not just the person. They would have the courage to realise that they are part of the 'problem' too. They would think about how they might be contributing to the issue and focus on what they could try to do differently. As the saying goes, '*If you always do what you always did you'll always get what you always got.*' So try doing something different yourself.

▌ They would look for some positives about the other person or people involved. What are they doing well? When are they not a problem? What have they done well in the past? What are they doing right now that is not a problem?

How would you feel if your boss was describing you as a problem?

Once you have established that the person is not all bad and useless, you can start to build on that more positive platform and arrive at much more effective outcomes.

Let's face it, you are not going to make things better by focusing on what a person does badly. You are not going to get them in a positive frame of mind to do something about the so-called problem by being negative and critical of them. They are just going to feel resentful. Whether they are at fault or not is pretty much irrelevant. The fact is, you are the manager and you need to understand and develop your skill in this area, so that you start to get the outcome and results you want. You certainly will not achieve them by becoming angry and critical.

Psychologists believe that a great deal of positive emotion is essential for creativity and for building effective relationships and networks. We also believe that these are key areas for successful organisations. The idea is that human beings are drawn towards the positive and away from the negative. So if you are able to focus more on the positives than the negatives in a person, you are likely to be regarded as a more effective manager.

There is another aspect of this theory, too. It is that our moods and behaviours are more affected by the negative than by the positive. So, for example, although people will be happy to receive praise, any criticism will have a greater and longer-lasting impact on them. We tend to remember criticism far more than any praise we are given. So you might unwittingly criticise someone and think nothing of it, but that will affect their behaviour and attitude towards you. You would then need to balance that by giving a higher amount of positive feedback.

According to research by Professor Marcial Losada, the ratio of positive to negative should be at the very least 3 to 1. He looked at 60 business organisations and measured their effectiveness in terms of profitability, customer satisfaction and employee attitudes. He found that for organisations to be effective, senior managers needed to do three things:

▌ Enquire more than they advocate. That means that they needed to ask more questions and do more listening rather than simply telling people what to do and giving advice.

▌ Be more positive than negative in their interactions. For really effective teams the ratio of positivity to negativity was more than 5 to 1. Just think about it for a moment: 5 to 1! You need to be giving five times as much positive feedback as negative feedback. How close is your ratio to that?

▌ Be more focused on others than on themselves.

So the question to ask yourself is: what is the ratio of positivity to negativity in your interactions? How much do I actually ask questions and listen to others, rather than simply putting forward my thoughts and opinions?

Interestingly, a ratio of 1 to 1 is not considered sufficient to make a difference. In fact, many of you might think that you don't even receive that much, and that you are actually getting more negative comments and feedback than positive ones. So perhaps aiming for a 1 to 1 ratio might be a start, but 3 to 1 should be your goal. Being more positive is one of the attributes of an effective leader and also leads to being more altruistic, more curious, more creative and more open to learning.

In case you are wondering whether it's ever ok to be negative and pessimistic, let us reassure you. The theory tells us that you should not usually go over a ratio of 10 positive to 1 negative. That would be considered unrealistically positive. It also tells us that your optimism should be flexible and that you need to be realistic. In other words, it can be ok to adopt a pessimistic approach when the costs of failure are high, or when talking to a person whose prospects are not good. In these cases you should not be over-optimistic but rather more realistic and point out the negative implications of what the person is doing.

> Being more positive is one of the
> attributes of an effective leader

How to respond constructively to others

Building and maintaining effective relationships isn't simply about remaining positive when things are going badly. How we respond to others' good news also affects our relationships. For example, if someone comes to you and tells you a piece of good news – let's say a promotion – you can respond in four basic ways. According to Professor Shelly Gable of the University of California, you

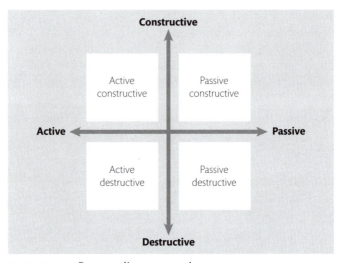

FIGURE 14.1 Responding to good news
Source: © Shelly Gable, used with permission

can respond either actively or passively, and you can be
either constructive or destructive. Let's look at the possible
combinations (see Figure 14.1).

▌ Active destructive

A negative way of responding is to be destructive and
this can be active or passive. So an active but destructive
response would be to focus on the negatives and say
something like, '*Oh, that's a lot of work to take on! Are
you sure you're ready for it?*'

What this is doing is belittling the other person and
questioning their capacity to succeed, but under the
pretence of being 'concerned' for them.

▌ Passive destructive

A passive-destructive response would be just to move
on to a completely different subject without even
acknowledging the promotion. Clearly this is not at all a

recommended approach, but aren't we all guilty of using it at times?

▌ Passive constructive

Clearly you would want to react in a constructive way, but even then it can be quite passive. So you might say something like, '*Well done!*', then move quickly onto another subject. This shows that although you might think you have been positive, you are in fact not really that interested in what the other person has to say. And the important thing here is the person will clearly understand that you're not that interested.

▌ Active constructive

What we would suggest is that you use the 'active-constructive' approach. So in this example you could say something like, '*That's excellent news. I know it means a lot to you!*' You would then ask some open questions about the job, or the person's feelings, or their plans for the new job. Or all of these! This then demonstrates clear interest in the other person, builds and strengthens your relationships and has the added benefit of contributing towards a more effective business.

The solution-focused way

The concept of solution focus and positive affirmations were introduced to us at a coaching workshop at the Brief Therapy Institute in London. After every practice session we were asked to turn to our colleagues and say something positive and affirmative to them. At first we found this extremely difficult. What to say? How to say it without sounding false? But after a shaky start we found we were able to notice and appreciate many things about the other person. And these were things that we would not have paid attention to previously. It became much easier and much more natural to express these things the more we did it.

We use something similar in our seminars at Ashridge. We put all the participants' names up on a wall chart and then ask everyone to write down something positive about all the other participants throughout the three days. We hand out Post-It notes and get people to stick them up on the board. Naturally it's a bit slow to start with, but things begin moving along as people take notice of what others are doing well, or are bringing to the sessions. Of course, not everything is positive, but we don't allow people to write down anything negative, just ask them to focus on the positives. What then happens is that at the end of the seminar everybody collects their positive affirmations, reads them and takes them home in an envelope.

We find that three things happen. One is that our participants really start to become more aware of others and notice much more than they did previously. Second, they start to become aware of their own positive contributions. And third, their energy level and confidence increase dramatically.

The other thing to remember is that it costs you absolutely nothing to do this. It's free! All it takes is a bit of attention to others, a positive perspective and the ability to appreciate rather than criticise. It's something any manager can do with their team.

Four key approaches to a solution-focused way of leading people

Find out what works and do more of it

As managers we are often focused on what is not working and then we can tend to criticise our people for not doing the right thing. But however well intentioned this is, it's not particularly helpful. Most people don't deliberately do things wrong, and if our reaction is to blame and criticise, it inevitably leads to defensiveness, excuses and cover-ups. So focusing on what is working leads to a very different type of conversation, one which is more open and productive, and therefore is positive and energising. Which then leads to more effective behaviours.

Create a clear idea of a better future

Many of you will be familiar with the idea of leaders creating a vision and then expecting their people to progress towards that vision. But the solution-focused approach to the future is not to try to envisage some far distant future towards which people will march, but rather to ask the people involved in the situation to create a positive image of a near future where things are better than they are at present. The idea is not to sell a specific preferred future but rather to engage people in what that future means for them – to get them actively involved in imagining what that future would look like specifically, then ask them what behaviours would start them on the road to that preferred future. This leads us to the next principle.

> Ask the people involved in the situation to create a positive image of a near future where things are better

Small steps

Leaders often want big and bold actions, but in the complex reality we are facing, these often founder and fail. The solution-focused approach would be to start small and use small steps in the right direction. This means that the process is often more realistic and more likely to succeed. The beauty of this approach is that everyone can be involved and capable of taking the small steps and then feel a sense of pride at achieving something. This is more effective than starting off too big and beating up yourself and others for failing. It's like our New Year resolutions to get fit and healthy. We set ourselves huge targets and goals and end up doing nothing. Far better to set a small target of doing something physical for, say, ten minutes a day and achieve that, than to set a target of running five miles every day and then failing to attain it. These small steps can be revisited and adapted, they are agile and nimble, and the great thing is that they can be reviewed frequently and adjusted as necessary. Contrast this with the major steps often asked for, which once started cannot be questioned.

Affirmations and compliments

The fourth key principle is twofold. It's about noticing what is working and then recognising and affirming it. You need to learn to spot useful things that people are doing and become used to seeing their strengths. Getting into the habit of doing that rather than focusing on weaknesses leads to a better working environment, good-quality relationships and improved performance.

It takes time to develop this positive habit, of course, especially if you are like most of us: good at noticing what is *not* working or going well. If you know that you are going to be appreciative then you learn to notice differently. You become more aware of what you like and value and what impresses you about someone and their work. You need to start being impressed with what people are doing and start to thank people as fellow human beings and not just in a robotic 'good job' type of way.

> You need to start being impressed with what people are doing

You might find the following reflective exercise useful – we learned it from colleagues at the Brief Institute.

Write down three things you are good at, at work. Then ask yourself, what else do I do well at work? Then ask yourself what else? What else? And what else? Keep on asking until you have at least 20 things written down. Look at the list. How does that make you feel? How easy was it?

If you found this exercise a little bit difficult, then we have just shown that you tend to find it hard to focus on positives rather than negatives. Would it have been easier if we had asked you to write down things you were bad at?

Why not use this exercise with your team – it can prove to be insightful.

Adopting positive approaches to leadership using the techniques we have described should contribute to your success and help you become highly regarded by your colleagues. These approaches lead to improved performance in the organisation and a better working climate. Unfortunately, it seems natural for us to focus on the negatives, on what is going wrong. We judge and criticise others easily. In fact, the ability to criticise seems like a part of our roles as managers. But people lose sight of the fact that the effect of criticism is a reduction in motivation, a loss of energy and low morale.

In our job as trainers, coaches and consultants working with managers from all sectors and countries, we see that this tendency to judge and criticise is deeply ingrained. New techniques such as the ones we mention above are trying to shift the focus away from criticism and help look at what people are doing well and what is actually working in organisations. This shift in focus improves morale and productivity.

This does not mean that we should never criticise anyone or never take faults and mistakes into account. It simply means that we need to balance our behaviour and try to consider what people are doing well, and develop the capacity to give constructive criticism in an effective way rather than simply focus on what they are doing badly. This approach is relatively easy to develop and will pay dividends by improving your skill as a people manager, so train yourself to look for what people are doing well. Then, having noticed it, point it out and praise the person for that specific aspect.

You can also encourage others to develop this capability by introducing appreciative feedback during team meetings.

One way of doing this would be at the end of the meeting to ask everyone to turn to the person on their left and tell them something they have appreciated about that person's contribution.

Tips for success

- Make sure your behaviour is balanced – in other words, focus on what's going well as well as what needs to improve.

- Develop the capacity to give constructive criticism.

- Don't simply focus on what people are doing badly.

- Train yourself to look for what people are doing well.

- Praise people for what they are doing well.

- Encourage others to be appreciative as well.

- Introduce appreciative feedback during team meetings.

And finally...

The most dangerous leadership myth is that leaders are born – that there is a genetic factor to leadership. That's nonsense; in fact, the opposite is true. Leaders are made rather than born.

Warren Bennis

People are at the heart of organisational life. Leading and getting the best out of your people will help contribute to the organisation's success. Leading people is a complex and challenging process. We hope that this book has introduced you to a number of tools, techniques and practices to help develop your people management and leadership skills. Now it's time to put it into practice and we would like to leave you with a few tips for the journey.

▌ Reputation is critical. Do you know what yours is?

▌ Take control of your career and life by developing a career plan.

▌ Develop resilience to cope effectively with setbacks, challenges and day-to-day problems.

▌ Develop and practise the art of coaching your people.

▌ Practise influencing without resorting to formal authority.

▌ Don't underestimate the importance of good facilitation skills to get the best out of your people.

▌ Know what motivates and demotivates both yourself and your team members.

■ Be clear about the performance you expect from others and ensure you know what is expected of you.

■ Learn how to leverage conflict and confrontation.

■ Understand the components of relational intelligence and work to develop them all.

■ Recognise that people often resist change for personal, emotional and psychological reasons.

■ Be aware of your own and your team's potential derailers.

■ Be appreciative, remember to look for the positive in others.

You completed this questionnaire earlier in this book, but you might like to complete it again having read the book, or at some point in the future in order to review your skill. For each of the areas we have suggested an additional book that will help you develop your skill further and will expand your knowledge of the area.

People management self-reflection quiz

People leadership areas	Skill/knowledge level 1 ----------4----------7	Development need: Low/med/high
Your skill set – being fully aware of your strengths, weaknesses and development needs		
The Leadership Skills Handbook (2012) by Jo Owen		
Your reputation – how others perceive you		
The Impact and Presence Pocketbook (2004) by Pam Jones, Jane Van Hooland and Phil Hailstone		

People leadership areas	Skill/knowledge level 1 ----------4----------7	Development need: Low/med/high
Resilience – your ability to deal with adversity and bounce back		
Bounce: Use the Power of Resilience to Live the Life You Want (2010) by Sue Hadfield and Gill Hasson		
Your career development – have a clear sense of your personal goals and plans		
What Colour is Your Parachute? (2012) by Richard N. Bolles		
Coaching – developing others to help them reach their full potential		
Coaching for Performance (2003) by John Whitmore		
Influencing – influences others to gain commitment and agreement to ideas and action		
The Leader's Guide to Influencing (2010) by Mike Brent and Fiona Elsa Dent		
Facilitation – acts as an enabler, involving others to ensure good-quality dialogue and outcomes		
Facilitating Groups (2010) by Jenny Rogers		

People leadership areas	Skill/knowledge level 1 -----------4-----------7	Development need: Low/med/high
Team building – developing and working with others to get things done for the benefit of the business		
Harvard Business Review on Building Better Teams (2011) *HBR*		
Motivation – creates a positive environment to get the best out of others		
Drive (2010) by Daniel Pink		
Performance management – sets goals and objectives for others and gives timely feedback		
Managing for Performance (2007) by Pam Jones		
Conflict management – deals effectively with interpersonal tensions		
Managing Conflict in the Workplace (2013) by Margaret and Shannon McConnon		

People leadership areas	Skill/knowledge level 1 ----------4----------7	Development need: Low/med/high
Relationship intelligence – manages and understands behaviour and emotions when working with others		
Social Intelligence (2011) by Daniel Goleman		
Change – understand the need for and implications of change and deliver successful outcomes		
Managing Transitions (2010) by William Bridges		
Derailment – awareness of the barriers, challenges and career derailers that could knock you off track		
The Elephant in the Boardroom (2010) by Adrian Furnham		
Positive leadership behaviour – using relational, appreciative and solution-focused processes to lead others		
The Solutions Focus (2011) by Paul Z. Jackson and Mark McKergow		

And finally...

People leadership areas	Skill/knowledge level 1 -----------4-----------7	Development need: Low/med/high
NOTES		

People management and leadership require significant understanding of people's psychology, together with a great deal of humility, flexibility and resilience. No one said it would be easy, but it's one of the most interesting journeys you can take. Don't hesitate to try things out – you can develop only by taking some risks – take small steps and get feedback at every opportunity.

Good luck.

References

Alderfer, C. (2012) *The Practice of Organisational Diagnosis: Theory and Methods.* Oxford University Press.

Argyris, C. (1993) *Knowledge for Action. A Guide to Overcoming Barriers to Organizational Change.* Jossey-Bass.

Argyris, C. (1992) *On Organizational Learning.* Blackwell.

Argyris, C. and Schon, D. (1978) *Organizational Learning.* Addison Wesley.

Ashridge Management Index 2012–2013., **www.ashridge. org.uk**.

Belbin, M. (2010) *Team Roles at Work.* 2nd edn. Butterworth-Heinemann.

Binney, G., Williams, C. and Wilke, G. (2012) *Living Leadership: A Practical Guide for Ordinary Heroes.* FT Publishing International.

Block, P. (2011) *Flawless Consulting: A Guide to Getting Your Experience Used.* John Wiley.

Bolles, R. N. (2012) *What Colour Is Your Parachute? 2013: A Practical Manual for Job Hunters and Career Changers.* Ten Speed Press.

Brent, M. and Dent, F. E. (2010) *The Leader's Guide to Influence.* FT Prentice Hall.

Bridges, W. (2009) *Managing Transitions. Making the Most of Change.* 3rd edn. NB Publishing.

Caplan, J. (2003) *Coaching for the Future.* CIPD.

Cialdini, R. (2007) *Influencing: The Psychology of Persuasion.* HarperBusiness.

Critchley, B., and Casey, D. (1984). 'Second Thoughts on Team Building.' *Management Education and Development*, Vol.15, Pt.2, pp163–175.

Conger, J. (2008) *The Necessary Art of Persuasion*. HBR.

Csikszentmihaly, M. (2002) *Flow: The Psychology of Happiness*. Rider.

Darwin, C. (1998) *The Origin of Species*. Wordsworth Editions.

Dent, F. E. (2009) *Working Relationships Pocketbook*. Management Pocketbooks.

Dent, F. E. and Brent, M. (2006) *Influencing Skills for Business Success*. Palgrave Macmillan.

Dent, F., Holton, V. and Rabbetts, J. (2013) *Ashridge Management Index*. Ashridge.

Ekman, P. (2003) *Unmasking the Face: A Guide to Recognising Emotions from Facial Expressions*. Malor Books.

Firth, D. and Leigh, A. (1998) *The Corporate Fool*. Capstone.

Flaherty, J. (1999) *Coaching – Evoking Excellence in Others*. Butterworth-Heinemann.

Frankl, V.E. (2000) *Man's Search for Ultimate Meaning*. Perseus.

Fredrickson, B. (2011) *Positivity*. Three Rivers Press.

French, J. and Ravens, B. (1958) 'The Bases of Social Power'. In D. Cartwright (ed.) *Studies in Social Power*. Institute of Social Research.

Furnham, A. (2010) *The Elephant in the Boardroom: The Causes of Leadership Derailment*. Palgrave Macmillan.

Gable, S., Gonzaga, G.C. and Strachman, A. (2006) 'Will you be there for me when things go right? Supportive responses to positive event disclosures.' *Journal of Personality and Social Psychology*, Vol. 91, No. 5, 904–917.

Gallwey, T. (2001) *The Inner Game of Work*. Random House.

Gardener, H. (2011) *Frames of Mind: The Theory of Multiple Intelligences*. Basic Books.

Garrat, B. (1983) 'The Power of Action Learning.' In M. Pedler (ed.) *Action Learning in Practice.* Gower.

Goldacre, B. (2009) *Bad Science.* Fourth Estate.

Goleman, D. (2007) *Social Intelligence: The New Science of Human Relationships.* Arrow.

Goleman, D. (2004) *Working with Emotional Intelligence.* Bloomsbury.

Goleman, D. (1996) *Emotional Intelligence.* Bloomsbury.

Goleman, D., Boyatzis, R. and Mckee, A. (2004) *Primal Leadership.* HBR Press.

Grint, K. (2005) *Leadership: Limits and Possibilities.* Palgrave Macmillan.

Hadfield, S. and Hasson, G. (2010) *Bounce: Use the Power of Resilience to Live the Life You Want.* Pearson Life.

Harvard Business Review (2011) *Harvard Business Review on Building Better Teams.* Harvard Business School Press.

Heron, J. (2001) *Helping the Client: A Creative Practical Guide.* Sage.

Heron, J. (1999) *The Complete Facilitator's Handbook.* Kogan Page.

Herzberg, F. (1993) *The Motivation to Work.* Transaction Publishing.

Hunt, J. (1992) *Managing People at Work.* McGraw-Hill.

Inglis, S. (1993) *Making the Most of Action Learning.* Gower.

Jackson, P. Z. and McKergow, M. (2007) *The Solutions Focus: Making Coaching and Change Simple.* NB Publishing.

Janssen, C. (2003) Personal conversation with authors.

Janssen, C. (1996) *The Four Rooms of Change. Forandringens Fyra Rum.* Wahlstromand Widstrand.

Jones, P. (2013*) Performance Management.* Pocket Books.

Jones, P. (2007) *Managing for Performance: Delivering Results through Others.* Pearson Business.

Jones, P. and Holton, V. (2006) *Teams Surviving in Complexity.* Ashridge.

Jones, P., Van Hool, J. and Hailstone, P. (2004) *The Impact and Presence Pocketbook.* Management Pocketbooks.

Joyce, P. and Sills, C. (2009) *Skills in Gestalt Counselling and Psychotherapy.* Sage.

Jung, C. G. (1990) *Analytical Psychology – Its Theory and Practice.* Ark Paperbacks.

Jung, C. G. (ed.) (1978) *Man and His Symbols.* Picador.

Jung, C. G. (1958) *Psychology and Religion.* Princeton University Press.

Jung, C. G. (1933) *Modern Man in Search of a Soul.* Harcourt Brace.

Katzenbach, J. and Smith, D. K. (2005) *The Wisdom of Teams.* McGraw-Hill.

Kets de Vries, M. (2001) *The Leadership Mystique.* Prentice Hall.

Kets de Vries, M. and Miller, D. (1984) *The Neurotic Organisation.* Jossey-Bass.

Kinlaw, D. (1999) *Coaching for Commitment.* Jossey-Bass/ Pfeiffer.

Lencioni, P. (2005) *Overcoming the Five Dysfunctions of a Team.* Jossey-Bass.

Losada, M. and Heaphy, E. (2004) 'The role of positivity and connectivity in the performance of business teams.' *American Behavioural Scientist*, Vol. 47, 740–65.

Macgregor, D. (1960) *The Human Side of Enterprise.* McGraw-Hill.

Maister, D. *et al.* (2002) *The Trusted Advisor.* Free Press.

Margerison, C. and McCann, D. (1995) *Team management – practical new approaches.* Management Books 2000.

Maslow, A. and Webb, D. (2013) *A Theory of Human Motivation.* Create Space IPP.

McCall, M. W. (1998) *High Flyers – Developing the Next Generation of Leaders*. Harvard Business School Press.

McConnon, M. and McConnon, S. (2010) *Managing Conflict in the Workplace*. How To Books.

McKergow, M. (2007) *Solution Focus Working*. Solutions Books.

McKergow, M. and Clarke, J. (eds) (2005) *Positive Approaches to Change*. Solutions Books.

Meharabian, A. (2007) *Non Verbal Communication*. Aldine Transaction.

Melville, N. (2013) Personal conversation with authors.

Molden, D. (2007) *NLP Business Masterclass*. FT Prentice Hall.

Nolan, V. (1989) *The Innovator's Handbook*. Sphere.

Nolan, V. (1981) *Open to Change*. MCB.

Owen, J. (2012) *The Leadership Skills Handbook: 50 Essential Skills You Need to Be a Leader*. Kogan Page.

Pedler, M. (ed.) (1983) *Action Learning in Practice*. Gower.

Pedler, M. *et al.* (1991) *The Learning Company: A Strategy for Sustainable Development*. McGraw-Hill.

Pink, D. (2011) *Drive: The Surprising Truth About What Motivates Us*. Cannongate Books Ltd.

Prince, G. M. (1970) *The Practice of Creativity*. Harper Row.

Robinson, D. and Hayday, S. (2009). Report No. 470, Institute for Employment Studies. Rogers, C. (2004) *On Becoming a Person*. Constable.

Rogers, J. (2010) *Facilitating Groups*. Open University Press.

Rosinski, P. (2003) *Coaching Across Cultures*. Nicholas Brealey Publishing.

Ruben, D. (1977) 'Guidelines for Cross-Cultural Communication Effectiveness.' *Journal of Group and Organisation Management*, Vol. 2, 470–9.

Schank, R. and Marsan, G. S. (1995) *Tell Me a Story: Narrative and Intelligence*. NUP.

Seligman, M. (2011) *Flourish. A New Understanding of Happiness and Well Being.* NB Publishing.

Seligman, M. (2003) *Authentic Happiness.* NB Publishing.

Senge, P. (2006) *The Fifth Discipline: The Art and Practice of the Learning Organisation.* Random House.

Thorndike, R. K. (1920) 'Intelligence and Its Uses.' *Harpers Magazine*, Vol. 140, 227–335.

Tomasello, M. (2010) *Origins of Human Communication.* MIT Press.

Tomasello, M. (2009) *Why We Cooperate.* MIT Press.

Tuckman, B. (1965) Developmental sequence in small groups. *Psychological Bulletin*, Vol. 63, No. 6, 384–99.

Ward, K. Kennedy, M. and Brent, M. (2002) *Making Complex Teams Work.* Ashridge.

Watkins, M. D. (2012) How managers become leaders. *Harvard Business Review*, June.

Wheatley, M. (1992) *Leadership and the New Science.* Berrett-Koehler.

Whitmore, J. (2003) *Coaching for Performance.* 3rd edn. Nicholas Brealey Publishing.

Index